D0208877

THE PHENOM
THE NEW TES

THE PHENOMENON
OF THE NEW
TESTAMENT

C. F. D. MOULE

SCM PRESS LTD

334 01345 3

First published 1967
by SCM Press Ltd
58 Bloomsbury Street
London WC1
Second impression 1981

Printed in Great Britain by
Richard Clay Ltd (The Chaucer Press)
Bungay, Suffolk

CONTENTS

PREFACE TO THE NEW IMPRESSION

There are those who deem it wrong-headed to engage in Christian apologetic at all; and a defence of Christianity claiming, not, indeed, that Christianity can be 'proved', but that there are rational grounds for taking this particular leap of faith rather than another, is probably no more in favour now than fourteen years ago when this book first appeared; but I do not repent of what I attempted. There are points, of course, at which my emphasis would be different were I writing it today, for I hope I have not stood still mentally – just as I hope that my style may have become less sententious over the years. But I am bound to say that I believe that its two main propositions still stand up.

First, the genesis of the Easter belief and of the Christian movement, which is an undoubted historical event, is impossible to describe plausibly without resort to the concept of revelation, which concerns what transcends history. Conversely, the tests of the validity of an alleged Christian revelation must include historical events. In other words, although history cannot cross its own frontier, it can conduct you to that frontier, and it can even point in the direction in which you should go beyond it.

Secondly, the understanding of Jesus Christ as more than individual, and yet the insistence that this inclusive Person is continuous with the historical individual, is a phenomenon in the New Testament which it is impossible to accommodate except within a distinctively Christian understanding of God.

Broadly speaking, too, the propositions of the two earlier papers reprinted here as appendices still seem to me to hold. There is, I still think, everything to be said for seeing 'the Son of Man' as Jesus' own choice of a symbol for his vocation and for that of his group; and for recognizing that the symbol stands for vindication in the court of Heaven only on the further side of suffering and death; and for acknowledging that neither does that symbol, in itself, include the idea of redemption, nor is there firm evidence that it was consciously combined by Jesus with Isaiah 53. The undoubtedly redemptive nature of the cross and the undoubted appropriateness of Isaiah 53 to its expression are not, in themselves, evidence that Jesus himself actually said much to this effect, still less that he said it in terms of Isaiah 53, whether or not combined with 'the Son of Man'. What I want to add now (and have added in various subsequent publications) is the observation that the all but uniform use of the definite article ('*the* Son of Man') in sayings attributed to Jesus must reflect a locution in the Aramaic tradition which was unequivocally deictic and meant '*the* Son of Man (that we know of from Daniel 7)'. The objection that the emphatic form in the Aramaic, *bar nasha*, would not have been unequivocally deictic only means that there must have been some other Aramaic locution that was. An exact parallel to the linguistic phenomenon I am postulating is presented by the Ethiopic of the Similitudes of Enoch (I Enoch 37–71), where the human figure is first introduced anarthrously and almost as a quotation from Daniel 7 (46.1, 'another being whose countenance had the appearance of a man'), but thereafter is always referred to as 'the' or 'that' or 'this Son of Man' (46.4; 62.5,7,9,14; 63.11; 69.26f.,29; 71.14,17).

As for the thesis of the second appendix, I believe more than ever that the Synoptic Gospels represent a conscious attempt to tell the pre-resurrection story in support of the apostolic preaching, rather than constituting a preaching of the full Easter belief or the full post-resurrection Christology of the Evangelists themselves; and to interpret the Synoptic Gospels as thus ancillary to the apostolic gospel makes a considerable difference to one's understanding of the emergence of Christian doctrine, and of the way in which Christology developed. It means that one ought not to assume a 'Synoptic Christology' as current in the early Church, alongside other Christologies.

Some of these proposals have since been independently endorsed, one way and another. J. D. G. Dunn's *Unity and Diversity in the New Testament* (SCM Press 1977) bears out the New Testament's maintenance of a continuity between Jesus of Nazareth and the Church's Lord. M. D. Hooker's *Jesus and the Servant* (SPCK 1959) and *The Son of Man in Mark* (SPCK 1967) both bear on the first appendix, as does my own essay, 'Neglected Features in the Problem of "the Son of Man" ' (J. Gnilka (ed.), *Neues Testament und Kirche* (Freiburg/Basel/Wien: Herder 1974), 413ff.), and J. Bowker's 'The Son of Man', *JTS* n.s. 28 (1977), 19ff., not to mention the huge spate of other studies on the subject. Innumerable books and essays relevant to various aspects of this book have appeared, but to acknowledge and discuss them would mean writing a new book.

Here there is space only to underline certain points and to modify others. Something that calls for underlining because it has been frequently misunderstood is the argument from success (pp. 11–13, 19, 43). Of course it is obvious that mere success is no criterion of truthfulness or authenticity, for plenty of movements whose tenets most thoughtful persons would reject flourish mightily. The argument from the survival of Christianity is nothing so naïve. The point is that in Christianity there was nothing besides the Easter belief to account for its survival or its differentiation from Judaism. It was not as though the Church offered any other novelties or advantages to its adherents over the Judaism of its time which might have carried an incidental error in a 'package deal' to success. Its survival was a test of nothing but the truth and the spiritual and moral effectiveness of its distinctive faith, for initially it was simply a sect of Judaism saying 'Jesus lives'. With this it stood or fell. That it stood is thus significant. Among statements that need modifying is that the Gospels represented a new literary genre. To this C. H. Talbert's *What is a Gospel? The Genre of the Canonical Gospels* (Philadelphia: Fortress Press, and SPCK 1977) constitutes a challenge – though this does nothing to reduce the originality of the contents of a Christian Gospel. Again, the late lamented J. Jeremias observed in his later work (e.g. *New Testament Theology* I, ET SCM Press 1971, 66) that *Abba* was after all not exclusively a child's word; but this does not alter the fact that it is an intimate word and seems to have been, till Jesus used it, unprecedented in prayer. The understanding of the Church as the Body of Christ is rarer in the New Testament than I had imagined. More often than not the body is used as an analogy for a harmonious society rather than being actually identified with Christ. But there are passages, nevertheless, where the identification is made; and, in any case, the Church's organic connexion with Christ is sufficiently evidenced in other ways. The interpretation of the brief Marcan form of the great commandment as uniquely significant has been challenged; but if it is unjustified, at any rate the argument does not depend upon this single point.

Gratefully, then, I accept the opportunity for a reprint of this little book. My gratitude to the President and Staff of Pittsburgh Theological Seminary for electing me to deliver the lectures which lay behind it has already been expressed in the original issue.

Easter 1981   C.F.D.M.

I

THE SECT OF THE NAZARENES

THIS book is really addressed to two groups of readers, though it can only hope, at best, to reach one of them. It is for those who have written off Christianity because they think that it is based on insufficient evidence; and for those who, while remaining Christians, feel discontented about some of the claims made for the authenticity of Christianity, or would be glad of help in reconsidering them. It is only the latter group that it is likely to reach directly; but it is possible that, through them, it may have some indirect impact on the former also. In either case, it has to admit to being intended as a small contribution to Christian apologetic; and this is an admission which at once lands the writer in an extremely uncomfortable position. A straight fight with opponents of Christian belief might be painful enough, but it would at least be an unambiguous contest. But anybody who presumes to set up as a Christian apologist has also to reckon with the fact that, within the body of Christian belief and among his own familiar friends, there are plenty by whom apologetic is today regarded as a very bad thing. It is so regarded not only because, tactically and psychologically speaking, organized defence is sometimes only another way of confessing defeat (*qui s'excuse s'accuse*); but also because of a great shift of emphasis that has come over the Church of recent years. It is no longer regarded as necessarily desirable to stand up for one's faith. If there is a fashionable virtue, it is rather in a self-effacing willingness to listen and give full value to the other man's faith. Christianity has so often fought for itself in the past, and so often won itself a name for blind dogmatism, that it is understandable if there is something of a revulsion at present. But more than that. There is the pressing question: What does apologetic imply about the nature of history in relation to Christian faith? Is not Christian faith something that not only does not need to defend itself, but

I

by definition cannot begin to produce evidence without ceasing to be faith? Is not Christian apologetic today ruled out as misconceived? Has not Karl Barth said that apologetic is the death of serious theology?

So the apologist is doubly suspect. And I must hasten to explain myself. I am not so foolish as to be trying to 'prove Christianity'. Neither am I so ignorant as not to have heard of the quest of the historical Jesus, and the *cul de sac* to which that once led.[1] I know, of course, that the scientifically demonstrable cannot, by definition, be the object of faith, and I am tolerably familiar with the extremely vehement debate still in progress about history and the gospel.

But here, I do confess that I take sides decidedly with those who emphasize that Christianity is a historical religion, and against those who say that the quest of the historical Jesus is irrelevant; and, in particular, I find myself driven, again and again, to take seriously the 'evidence'—if that is the right word—for what Christian belief calls the resurrection. And I therefore unashamedly address myself to those who are prepared to allow to historical evidence a place in the considerations leading up to faith. And among such persons, I should like especially to catch the ear—even if it is only indirectly, through those who read this book—of those who fancy that the origins claimed by Christianity for itself can be explained away and that they present no problem for the serious historian.

One of the reasons which move me to wish to do this is that, among those who oppose or neglect Christian evidence, a strangely perverse attitude is often to be found. This is the attitude which, while quite unwarrantably hospitable to the latest irresponsible speculation by the journalistic charlatans, insists on treating such serious documents as those which comprise the New Testament as though they had long ago been discredited. I have met otherwise intelligent men who ask, apparently in all seriousness, whether there may not be truth in what I would call patently ridiculous legends about (let us say) an early portrait of Jesus or

[1] As long ago as 1892, Martin Kähler's now famous book, *Der sogenannte historische Jesus und der geschichtliche, biblische Christus*, announced: 'I regard the entire Life-of-Jesus movement as a blind alley' (translation by C. E. Braaten, *The So-called Historical Jesus and the Historic, Biblical Christ*, 1964, 46). This was well before Albert Schweitzer's book, *Von Reimarus zu Wrede*, 1906.

the shroud in which he is supposed to have been buried (I am thinking of actual articles in the popular press), and who grow excited over the Gospel of Thomas or some other late apocryphal document, but who brush aside the much earlier and more sober canonical Gospels as unreliable legends not worthy of serious consideration.

Another reason for taking the line I do is quite simply that, within its strict limits, I believe it is valid, and yet seldom pursued. The point is that I am not attempting here to reconstruct 'the Jesus of History', either in the biographical manner which was exposed by Albert Schweitzer as a mistaken effort and is now almost universally abandoned, or, in the manner which is beginning now to become fashionable in certain circles, in terms of his message and the impact of his person upon his own hearers and observers—although I shall be touching on this incidentally. All I am trying to do is to present certain undoubted phenomena of the New Testament writings and to ask how the reader proposes to account for them. If the coming into existence of the Nazarenes, a phenomenon undeniably attested by the New Testament, rips a great hole in history, a hole of the size and shape of Resurrection, what does the secular historian propose to stop it up with? If a Jewish writer like Paul speaks of a contemporary, Jesus of Nazareth, in language up to that time used only in reference to great symbolic figures of the remote past, what account are we to give of the processes leading to this? And so forth. It seems to me that opponents of Christianity are allowed too easily either to avoid such questions altogether or to get round them with shallow speculations which do not really survive scrutiny. It is phenomena of this sort that I propose to examine, inviting interested students to join in the examination and then to talk about it with others. 'Christianity', writes D. E. Jenkins,[2] 'is based on indisputable facts. . . . I do not say that Christianity is the indisputable interpretation of these facts.' It is precisely some of these indisputable facts that I here present, asking whether the Christian interpretation, though I agree that it is not indisputable, is not by far the most plausible—almost (I would venture to think) the inescapable—interpretation.

[2] D. E. Jenkins and G. B. Caird, *Jesus and God*, 1965, 26.

The Limits of the Inquiry

All this being said, I must emphasize the strict limits of the inquiry. At best, this is only a tiny contribution, in one small corner of Christian apologetic. But of course, as I have already said, this one small corner is a storm-centre. To handle the New Testament means running against the thorny question of *the meaning of history*. Despite himself, the simple investigator gets betrayed into taking sides philosophically. What, for instance, is the meaning of these two statements of alleged fact: (i) the tomb in which Jesus had been laid was found empty; (ii) Jesus was seen alive after his death? Are they both of the same type, as allegedly historical statements? Or is the first theoretically capable of verification (supposing we had been there and could have investigated) while the second is not (and no amount of weighing and measuring could ever establish it)? Again, to what extent do value-judgments enter in? Would it be true to answer, in the first case, not at all—for the tomb was either empty or it was not—but in the second, very much indeed? And what, once again, is the relative importance of the two for Christian evidence? Would it be true to say of the first—the empty tomb—that its importance is relatively slight, and of the second that it is paramount? Please note that I am not here committing myself to an answer—only indicating problems.

For such are some of the problems that, involuntarily, one encounters by implication, even if not explicitly. But I am not going to pursue them immediately. What I mean to do, having registered my awareness of such problems, and my recognition that I am bound to be involved in them, if only by implication, is to start from certain incontestable facts, namely, certain ways in which the Christians themselves demonstrably wrote about Jesus, and to ask the critic of Christianity how he proposes to account for them. But, before that, I must add here yet two more preliminary observations relating to Christian apologetic.

Preliminary Observations

(i) *The need for humility towards others' convictions*

First, I am deeply aware that one of the most important sides of evangelism is the Christian's humility before the facts and his readiness to welcome an opponent's questions, to listen atten-tively, and take them seriously: to enter, in other words, into genuine dialogue. And I should be distressed indeed if these chapters conveyed the impression that I am forgetting this, or that my idea of Christian apologetic is intolerant or aggressive. I am only anxious that the unbeliever—the unbeliever within us who read, or the unbeliever with whom we may converse—should, sooner or later, be squarely faced with what, I think, are very hard questions indeed; that our Christian humility should be real, not craven; and that the Christian case should not be allowed to go by default. If at any point I sound assertive, I beg the reader to remember what I have just said.

(ii) *Demonstration is not evangelism*

Secondly, I know, as we all do, that argument is, even at its best, only a small part of evangelism, and often comes, if at all, at a late stage in the process. A review, in the London *Times* for 10 February 1966, of C. S. Lewis' *The Screwtape Letters* (first published in 1942), in a series entitled 'How well have they worn?', contains the following words:

> If Screwtape had read a later theology he would hardly have been afraid of humanity's *reasoning* itself into faith. An existentialist devil would have attacked not his victim's rationality, but his power of choice, his capacity for taking the leap. Or have persuaded his prey into a systematic, rational belief only to subvert it with the terrifying actuality of the absurd. But Screwtape seems to have been convinced by Chesterton—too easily it may seem to a later generation. . . . Screw-tape, like so many apologists, is preaching only to the converted.

I take the reviewer's point. Rational conviction, even when it can be had, is very different from commitment. W. Künneth, writing about the resurrection, says:

> The Christological question does not arise in the sphere of history pure and simple, but on its frontier, inasmuch as in the fact of Christ there emerges something absolutely unconditional, which is accessible only to faith.[3]

Commitment to Christ is a matter for the entire person, not for his mind alone; and intellectual conviction (if, indeed, it can be

---

[3] W. Künneth, *The Theology of the Resurrection*, ET 1965 of *Theologie der Auferstehung* (1951 edition). Cf. A. Richardson, *History Sacred and Profane*, 1964, 206: 'Christian theology has never suggested that the "fact" of Christ's resurrection could be known apart from faith.'

had at all without the whole person being involved) is not the whole business. But the whole business, precisely because it concerns the whole person, can never be achieved in defiance of the intellect. Reason, though not the whole, is a part of the personal response; and the attempt to bring to light the falseness of certain allegedly rational objections is therefore not unimportant. So much by way of preamble.

Some Popular Objections to the Christian View

The various approaches to the subject that I wish to offer will, I hope, become clearer as we go along. But, by way of introducing the first phenomenon or incontestable fact—namely, the emergence of the Christian Church, carrying with it the question, What launched 'the sect of the Nazarenes'?—let me try to assemble a few of the doubts and difficulties that I have actually heard expressed from time to time, from outside Christian belief, by both the thoughtful and the less thoughtful. One of the problems of Christian apologetic is to make itself audible at all to those who have never studied its position. The objections are often very crude and elementary and disclose a total misunderstanding of the very claims that are being defended, even when the objector is a highly educated person. Consequently, the claims are often allowed simply to go unexamined; and those of us who already accept them must remember this lack of contact with those who do not, and must remember the crudity of some of the objections. That is my only reason for spending time now on the extremely naïve objections to the Christian view which follow. Here, then, are some specimens of attempts to 'explain away' this phenomenon of the emergence of 'the sect of the Nazarenes'.

(i) *The resuscitation theory*

One conversation I recall rather clearly, with a man of high distinction in non-theological academic and public life. Like so many others, he had begun to feel deeply dissatisfied with the resurrection narratives of the Gospels—so contradictory, so hazy, to him so unconvincing. He had begun seriously to wonder whether the best explanation of the rise of Christianity was not, after all, the old resuscitation theory: that Jesus never actually died on the cross, but somehow managed to pull through. Pilate, you recall, expressed surprise that he should be already dead. The accounts suggest that Jesus was not always readily recognizable when he reappeared to his friends: perhaps, then, this means that he was veiled, so as to conceal the pallor of a man struggling back to life after the appalling ordeal he had survived. . . . And so on.

I do not say that this is any longer a very common type of criticism. For the most part it is self-defeating, because it uses, in the interests of its very doubts, details which, on its own showing, would be unlikely ever to have survived in the narratives. For if the Christians were so thoroughly hoodwinked by this pale survivor, it is unlikely that their accounts would be close enough to reality to have retained the tell-tale details. No doubt tell-tale details can be extremely important, and—as we shall see—can be fruitfully used in New Testament research. M. Bloch was absolutely right in pointing out that what he calls 'the evidence of witnesses in spite of themselves'[4] is of particularly high value. Of course; for it is, by definition, free from tendentious adjustment. But the resuscitation theory would make it necessary to postulate that the Gospel resurrection stories were such sheer romance that this type of evidence would scarcely appear in them at all.

But, in any case, how wildly improbable that such a Jesus could have launched the Church! And how incredible that, when the time for his death did ultimately come, he should have somehow eluded his friends so that his real death left no trace in their convictions! To this death, at least, one would think they would be bound to bear witness 'despite themselves'. No: most objectors to the Christian position are more likely to regard the movement as based on sheer fantasy or on hallucination than on a misinterpreted physical survival.[5] But I mention this line of argument because it was actually expressed in my hearing by a very intelligent person, and it is at least one of the attempted replies to our question, 'How do you explain this Sect of the Nazarenes?'

(ii) *The creation of Christology by current ideas*

Two other suggestions, made from time to time in the course of the centuries, have been tried again recently. Both depend upon

[4] *The Historian's Craft*, ET, 1954, of *Apologie pour l'histoire ou métier d'historien*, 1949.
[5] See the brief survey of alternative theories in A. Richardson, *History, Sacred and Profane*, 106 ff.

the theory that the Christian view of Jesus is a Christological myth, created simply by deep-seated traditional beliefs.

Prosper Alfaric, to take a fairly recent example, believed that a Jewish messianic expectation was enough to account for the creation of a legend about a Jesus who had never, in fact, existed. In his autobiography,[6] he tells the story of his life, from his birth on 21 May 1876, up to the time of his Professorship at Strasbourg which began in 1919, and of his pilgrimage from the Roman Catholic faith to agnosticism; and in the epilogue, he alludes to the view he had reached about Christian origins. In a lecture at the Sorbonne in 1946, entitled 'Les origines sociales du christianisme', Alfaric derived Christianity, as a messianic myth, from the Essenes.[7] Shortly afterwards came the Qumran documents, which Alfaric hailed as supporting his thesis, and more recently he has been followed in this respect by one or two others, who have tried to derive Christianity from Qumran.

The other type of derivation-theory does not deny the existence of Jesus, but explains the exalted Christian estimate of him simply by the world of thought belonging to Christian thinkers. Thus, H. J. Schoeps of Erlangen,[8] a learned Jewish student of Christian origins, tries to explain Paul's Christology by a mixture of Jewish traditional beliefs and Hellenistic speculations. He holds that Paul, in a completely new way, combined three Jewish ideas—the meaning of suffering and of a vicarious atoning sacrifice, the picture of the suffering servant of God in Isa. 53, and the binding of Isaac—and that, to this combination, he added certain heathen mythological conceptions, filtered through the Hellenistic syncretism of the time.[9] But neither of these theories begins to explain what it was that 'triggered off' the alleged process.

(iii) *Deliberate propaganda*

There are other speculations to be recorded. A popular approach which I have met in conversation is by the extraordinary

[6] *De la foi à la raison : scènes vécues*, Publications de l'Union Rationaliste, Paris, 1955.

[7] For other Jesus-myth theories, see J. Peter, *Finding the Historical Jesus*, 1965, 24, n. 2. Alfaric's *Pour comprendre la vie de Jésus* 1929, there noted, was not available to me.

[8] Cf. J. Klausner, and the criticism of his position by W. G. Kümmel in *Heilsgeschehen und Geschichte* (collected papers, Marburg, 1965), especially 173 ff.

[9] See H. J. Schoeps, *Paulus: die Theologie des Apostels im Lichte der jüdischen Religionsgeschichte*, 1959: ET, *Paul*, 1961, chapter 4.

theory that Peter, or some other strong personality, decided that it would be salutary to put about the idea that Jesus was alive, in order to bolster morale. 'You can have a salutary ethic' (so I suppose the astonishing argument must run) 'without the Christian Gospel. But if the Christian Gospel can be propagated, it may act as an added incentive: so let us propagate the Gospel of the resurrection! It will do good!' I submit that, if Christians today tried to support any of *their* claims by so ludicrously feeble a motive, they would be instantly laughed out of court. Something with more probability, as well as more vitality, than so stupid and insipid a calculated lie is needed to account for the origin and survival of the Church. Indeed, it is difficult to imagine that any responsible historian would seriously entertain any form of the 'pious fraud' theory—whether it be a fraud by Jesus (surviving death, but pretending that he had died and been raised), or by some disciple (falsely claiming to have seen the risen Master).

(iv) *Genuine misapprehension*

What is more widely believed, so far as I can ascertain, is that the Christian Church took its rise not indeed from a deliberate falsehood but from a sheer, honest misapprehension—assisted, perhaps, by superstitious awe and hallucination. For some reason (which, it is presumed, may be psychologically explained) these men and women became mistakenly convinced that their adored leader was alive again. A hoary old theory such as that the women went to the wrong tomb,[10] or (a theory that was known as long ago as St Matthew's Gospel) that the body was surreptitiously taken from the tomb, is still sometimes revived. On this showing, some of them genuinely found an empty tomb—emptied by some rationally explicable means unknown to them—which, it is suggested, assisted their belief that Jesus had risen. For, after all (it is urged), the traditions do say that Jesus himself predicted his resurrection; so that, even if the disciples were temporarily shaken by the disastrous death, it is hardly surprising if courage returned into their consciousness and they began to rally: they remembered the predictions; hope reasserted itself; the wish became father to the thought; he *must* have risen again—he *had* risen again: Alleluia! the Lord *is* risen indeed!

[10] See K. Lake, *The Historical Evidence for the Resurrection of Jesus Christ*, 1907.

One wonders whether those who light-heartedly advance this theory have thought hard about its difficulties[11]: but there it is—and, indeed, perhaps it is the best alternative, however lame, to the Christian account of the matter.

Christianity, on this showing, is to be explained by sincerely believed delusions, reinforced (we must add) by the comfort and security-value of so reassuring a faith. For good value, one can throw in the observation that it was coupled also with a great deal of moral goodness and warm fellowship which anyone might recognize as genuine, and which helped to lend momentum to the movement and make it attractive.

The Peculiar Problem of Christian Beginnings

Well, no Christian is going to deny that many an influential and vigorous movement has begun from a mistaken view of things and has survived and grown and prospered—provided always that the mistake contains enough of truth, or corresponds sufficiently to basic human needs or to the needs of the moment, or has a leader forceful enough, for it to gain momentum. But it is precisely here that Christianity is different. That is the main contention of this first chapter. Non-Christian Judaism, maintaining (mistakenly, as Christians think) the rejection of Jesus, continues to flourish, if only because of the deep bed-rock of positive truth in its worship of one righteous, personal God.[12] Islam, for all its errors and delusions (as Christians deem them), thrives not only on its nationalist and traditionalist *élan,* but, at least in part, on the truth and deep piety of its religious convictions at their best. Marxist Communism is an ideology which stands for certain deeply true human principles, even if its rejection of the supernatural and its rigid doctrines of historical evolution are, in the estimation of many, fundamental mistakes.

---

[11] '. . . those who propound the psychological theories of the resurrection of Jesus usually fail to admit to the monstrous character of the interpretation of history which their theories have inevitably, if inadvertently, created'— R. R. Niebuhr, *Resurrection and Historical Reason,* 1957, 179. See, further, a discussion of such theories by A. R. C. Leaney in *Vindications* (edited A. Hanson), 1966, 130 ff.

[12] H. J. Schoeps, *Paul,* 256 f., says, strikingly: '. . . the continued existence of Israel almost 2,000 *post Christum natum,* still undisturbed in its consciousness of being God's covenant people, is testimony that the old covenant has not been abrogated, that as the covenant of Israel it continues to exist alongside the wider human covenant of the Christian Church.'

Why, then, should Christians claim an any more 'objective' beginning for their faith? May not Christianity be one more movement precipitated by a delusion but kept going by certain general, permanent truths and virtues?

Christianity had this Conviction alone as its Raison D'Être: *with this it Stood or Fell*

The short answer to that question is that what is alleged to have been a delusion was the first Christians' sole *raison d'être*: they had nothing else to lend momentum to the launching, or to prevent their simply losing their identity thereafter. As W. Künneth writes:

the primitive Christian message . . . did *not* make general statements about Jesus, but concentrated upon definite happenings, and brought out one singular event as the essential content of faith and as the ground of faith.[13]

This is the heart of my contention. This alleged delusion has got to be strong enough (for they began with nothing else that was distinctive) to launch this 'sect', and tenacious enough to keep up their distinctiveness over against the pious Judaism to which they otherwise belonged.[14]

From the very first, the conviction that Jesus had been raised from death has been that by which their very existence has stood or fallen. There was no other motive to account for them, to explain them. They had no 'ideology' to proclaim, like so many other movements—Islam with its passionate monotheism, Marxism with its fanatical hatred of capitalism. G. E. Ladd writes:

They had no fixed teachings like the disciples of the rabbis. They had no new *halachah* or legislation like the Pharisees. They had no evident organization. As Dahl has forcefully put it, 'the fellowship of Jesus' disciples was something strange within Judaism: a separate synagogue without a synagogue and without halachah! An apocalyptic

---

[13] *The Theology of the Resurrection*, 117.
[14] The argument which I here try to develop is, I think, independent of, though complementary to, that which concentrates on original eye-witness to the risen Christ and the subsequent confirmation of the fact of the risen Christ throughout the Church's history (see e.g. Leaney, *Vindications*, 129 f.). I am concentrating more narrowly on the historian's question: What triggered off the Church in the first instance? But the answer which I find points also beyond history.

circle without an apocalyptic teaching! A messianic movement without the ardour of the zealots.'[15]

They shared with Judaism its monotheism, its personal conception of religion, its splendid ethics of family life; but this was not what they preached as their distinctive message; and in proportion as they did share these things with the Jews it is only the harder to explain how they gained and then maintained their distinctiveness. What does explain it is the resurrection.

To the Christians, then, belonged none of the main *raisons d'être* which help to explain other groupings. In the passage just quoted from G. E. Ladd, he goes on:

The one thing which bound them together was their personal relationship to Jesus and his message about the Kingdom of God.

But I question (and I think Dr Ladd would himself agree with me) whether this personal relationship and this message mean anything without the resurrection. The Christians were not a society gathered round the memory of a beloved Master of former days. They did, of course, cherish the memory of Jesus; but not with the biographical care of a backward-looking group of admirers. Neither, as I have said, were they primarily the bearers of a new ethic or a new way of life. Christianity did indeed find itself, in due course, led into a new attitude to all sorts of problems, and did evolve a characteristic ethic; but that was not its starting-point or its distinctiveness. In the course of time the Christian Church has, undoubtedly, acquired certain features alien to its distinctive basis. By alien features, I do not, I hasten to say, mean an involvement in 'the world'. On the contrary, most of its failure lies precisely in an insufficient 'involvement' of the right kind. The sort of alien accretions I have in mind belong rather to legalizing and systematizing and a negative contracting out of 'the world' and so forth. But anyway, whether good or bad, none of these additions or alterations helps to explain why the Church ever started, nor how it maintained its distinctiveness in the early years against the natural tendency to revert to Judaism. This is the phenomenon which, I am claiming, should be pushed before the critic again and again. Where did the Gospel—the Gospel of the resurrection—spring from? How, indeed, did that new literary form we call a Gospel ever come into being?

[15] *Jesus and the Kingdom*, New York, 1964; London, 1966, 251. The quotation is from N. A. Dahl, *Das Volk Gottes*, 1941, 161.

Thus, neither of the most obvious main motives—neither the ideological nor the sentimental—is *discernible to the historian investigating Christian origins*; and the birth and rapid rise of the Christian Church therefore *remain an unsolved enigma for any historian who refuses to take seriously the only explanation offered by the Church itself.*[16]

The Latter-Day Saints no Parallel

One other alleged parallel might here be mentioned. Those who think that Christianity can be explained as just an early specimen of the recurrent phenomenon of deluded sects, might well be tempted to point to the rise of the Latter-Day Saints, commonly called the Mormons. But I would repeat, there is a uniqueness in the Christian *articulus stantis et cadentis ecclesiae*—that by which the Church stands or falls. Christianity stood or fell by its conviction of the resurrection of a figure of history, Jesus of Nazareth. Mormonism (so far as I can see) took its rise (apart from its biblical background which, to that extent, makes it only a derivative from Christianity) round the alleged revelations to Joseph Smith: that is, round a series of injunctions and generalizations. The only *event* it could appeal to was the alleged discovery of the golden book. And even if this had been a reality, and not an hallucination or a hoax, it is still the content of the book, not the event of its discovery, that constitutes (so far as I can see) essential Mormonism. No doubt in fact the sect owed its origin in large measure also to the impressive though deranged personality of Joseph Smith himself, and to the surrounding atmosphere of extravagant sectarianism. But neither in the contents of the book nor in the personality of its founder is there any parallel that might help, by analogy, to explain the rise of Christianity, which was not a sect with new doctrines to propagate, nor the circle of a dominating prophet, but a body of people bearing witness to the alleged resurrection of an historical figure.

Alleged parallels from the history of the sects, judging by this, are unlikely to be any more satisfactory than that of the great world-religions, as analogies for the peculiar origin of Christianity.

[16] 'Naturalizing the gospel history', says R. R. Niebuhr (in a critique of Renan), 'only succeeds in making it sentimental.' *Resurrection and Historical Reason*, 1957, 15.

The Evidence is from the Whole New Testament

Now, the peculiar character of the origin of Christianity to which I have been alluding is written large all over the New Testament. It is clearly enough exposed in the Acts. But it is not as though this conclusion emerges only from the reading of the Acts. There are many who would challenge the evidence of this book as a comparatively late and tendentious document, and a piece of Christian propaganda. For my part, I am very slow to believe that the writer of the Acts has played so fast and loose with his evidence as is sometimes supposed—not because I hold any theory of the moral perfection or the verbal infallibility of these Christians, but because what the author says is, for the most part, coherent and shows no internal evidence of serious distortion. But even if we were to write off this document as a distorted presentation of Christian preaching, it is still impossible to escape the evidence of those earlier documents, the Pauline epistles, and of all the rest of the New Testament. At no point within the New Testament is there any evidence that the Christians stood for an original philosophy of life or an original ethic. Their sole function is to bear witness to what they claim as an event—the raising of Jesus from among the dead.

Not Mere Restoration

It is, mark well, *raising*, and it is the raising of *Jesus*. This is what the Church stands or falls by. It is not simply a restoration to the old life, but a raising, an exaltation. Nor is it the raising of just anybody, but of the one who Jesus was. It is the recognition of the raising of the one who Jesus was, and the recognition of his raising as the *ultimate* and irreversible raising ('Christ, being raised from death, is never to die again', Rom. 6.9), and the recognition of Jesus as not *only* an individual but also as 'ultimate man' ('as in Adam all die, even so in Christ shall all be made alive', I Cor. 15.22). The estimate of Jesus as *designated Son of God* by the resurrection (Rom. 1.4) and as representative of all men is at the heart of this conviction, and is a constant element in the New Testament interpretation of Jesus. It is there by implication, as I shall argue in the next chapter, even when it is not explicit. It is part of the recognition of the resurrection as transcending time. W. Künneth writes:

The dimension of the resurrection of Jesus has a structure of its own, which is incommensurable with the forms in which other dimensions are expressed. A consequence of this is the often overlooked *difference of the resurrection from the miracles in history*. An identification of the resurrection with the preceding and succeeding miracles in the history of salvation, especially with the raising of the dead by Jesus himself, is accordingly no longer possible—however true it may be . . . that there is an inner connection between them.[17]

And again:

On the one hand, being itself an event related to history, it can give an answer to the question which history poses; on the other hand, as a reality that transcends history, it possesses the unconditional and universal quality necessary to what gives meaning.[18]

And again:

. . . the historic is not destroyed by the resurrection, but rather taken up into a new reality. The resurrection of Jesus is therefore not an abstract supra-historicality, but a concrete fulfilment of history.[19]

Similarly, A. R. C. Leaney writes:

For the Church, if the Resurrection is thought of as an event, it is an event which fills all time and which confronts every Christian as a spiritual reality.[20]

I say, then, again, that *whereas* within the New Testament there is much condemnation of vice, and a certain amount of exhortation to virtue, both of which any pious Jew, and a good many of the pagan moralists too, would have endorsed; *whereas* within the New Testament community there was a warmth and effectiveness of social relationship which other religions have emulated and would have been glad to rival, *yet* the elements in the New Testament which a non-Christian would not share are precisely the ones which alone account for the Church's existence. They are those which relate to and depend on the Christian estimate of Jesus as crucified and raised from among the dead, and of man's relationship to God through him.

The Old Testament Antecedents only point to the Newness

Not that even this, for all its novelty, was rootless or without genealogy. The way had been paved by certain aspects of

---

[17] W. Künneth, *The Theology of the Resurrection*, 79.
[18] *Op. cit.*, 249.   [19] *Op. cit.*, 253.   [20] *Vindications*, 129.

pre-Christian Jewish thought. The prophets of the pre-exilic period had taught God's initiative and his Covenant with Israel, and man's utter dependence on God's unmerited goodness; and this conviction and this attitude had been caught and repeated in the subsequent religious literature of the Hebrews, including (to mention an example much in our minds over the last few years) some passages in the Dead Sea Scrolls of Qumran.[21] A famous passage in the Book of Jeremiah had looked forward to a new and better Covenant one day (Jer. 31.31). But the conviction that this graciousness of God and this New Covenant are both mediated and embodied in Jesus of Nazareth was startlingly new. That Jesus is the fulfilment of past ideals and therefore their climax is an astonishing conviction. The Old Testament Scriptures had much to say of the achieving of God's purposes through the leadership of a chosen official, king or priest; or through the loyal obedience of a minority, even to the extent of suffering and martyrdom. But quite new was the interpretation of Scripture in such a way that all these symbols and figures were believed to converge and coalesce in a single figure of history—a figure of recent history, and he a condemned and disgraced criminal. The notion of the 'fulfilment' of the Scriptures in a single individual, who was claimed to be the coping-stone of their whole structure and the $\tau\acute{\epsilon}\lambda o s$ or goal of God's whole design, was new; and it was the Christian community that first related together, round this single focus, the scattered and largely disconnected images of Israel's hope. Even if here two and there three of these images had begun to coalesce in earlier aspiration,[22] it was utterly new for them all to be clustered together round an historical figure. Christians are familiar enough with the idea that 'Messiah', 'Christ', 'Son of God', 'Son of Man', 'Suffering Servant', and 'Lord' are interchangeable terms all relating to one figure. But I

[21] E.g. 1QS 11.2^b, 3: 'For, as for me, my judgment is with God and in his hand is the perfection of my way; with him is the uprightness of my heart 3 and in his righteousness he will blot out my transgressions.' Cf. 1QH 15.12 f.: 'I know through the understanding which comes from Thee that righteousness is not in a hand of flesh, [that] man [is not master of] his way and that it is not in mortals to direct their step.' (The quotation from 1QS is from A. R. C. Leaney, *The Rule of Qumran and its Meaning*, 1966, 235; that from 1QH is from G. Vermès, *The Dead Sea Scrolls in English*, 1962, 194.)

[22] See W. Zimmerli and J. Jeremias, *The Servant of God*, ET, SBT 20, 1957 (revised edition, 1965); and a valuable discussion in D. S. Russell, *The Method and Message of Jewish Apocalyptic*, 1964, 334 ff.

know of no evidence that this situation had been precipitated until the Christ-event.

Two other matters relating to the novelty of the impact of the Christian convictions on Scripture are relevant to this stage in our argument. First, a good case can be made for the belief that the interpretation of Scripture three-dimensionally (as one might say) is new, and goes back to Jesus himself. Philonian allegory treats Scripture two-dimensionally and therefore arbitrarily: for Philo it is a plane surface from any part of which something may be picked out and arbitrarily made to bear an allegorical significance. Similarly the verbal conceits of rabbinic exegesis, for all their show of loyalty to the letter, were essentially fanciful, arbitrary and uncontrolled—or, if controlled, controlled only by tradition, not by any historical data. And equally arbitrary is the much discussed *pesher*-technique of the Qumran Habakkuk scroll, which takes a passage in a prophet and declares that the *pesher*, or interpretation, of it is so-and-so (alluding to current events).[23] Neither can one deny that these methods of using Scripture can all be paralleled from the New Testament: they can, and nobody can deny that Christians took them over. But what is distinctive of the New Testament, over and above inherited techniques for the use of the Hebrew Scriptures, is the genuinely 'three-dimensional', historical use of them, as a record of God's dealings with his people and thus as an index of God's ways of achieving his purpose. When this new attitude to Scripture is adopted, and the man from Nazareth is found at the convergence of all the lines of historical perspective, one is bound to recognize something startlingly novel, and to ask what there is to account for it. And the answer seems to be a most powerful and original mind, and a tremendous confirmatory event.[24]

And secondly, it is in the New Testament that a new and creative conception of suffering comes into the centre of the picture. There are in the Old Testament a few hints of this notion, but they are rare. It is full of suffering and heroic endurance, but far less full of the confidence that suffering thus borne may be actually creative. Isa. 53 is almost alone in the Old

[23] E.g. 1Qp Hab. 2.12 (on Hab. 1.6ᵃ): 'Interpreted, this concerns the Kittim who are quick and valiant in war, causing many to perish. . . .' G. Vermès, *The Dead Sea Scrolls in English*, 1962, 233.

[24] See e.g. C. H. Dodd, *According to the Scriptures*, 1952, 110.

Testament in this respect. Very strangely, that particular passage is only sparingly used in the New Testament.[25] But even without it, a conception of the death of Christ as not only triumphant but positively redemptive of others does become formulated.[26] It is better to say that Jesus is 'about Isa. 53' than that Isa. 53 is 'about Jesus': and this is a phenomenon not lightly to be brushed aside when we pose the question: How explain the Nazarenes?

Thus, to return to the main contention, it may be demonstrated, I think, from such comparisons of the New Testament with Jewish literature generally, that the Christian interpretation of Scripture, as well as being remarkably original (in what it added to all the traditional techniques), points to the one great distinguishing mark of Christianity. It is another way of saying that the one really distinctive thing for which the Christians stood was their declaration that Jesus had been raised from the dead according to God's design, and the consequent estimate of him as in a unique sense Son of God and representative man, and the resulting conception of the way to reconciliation.

We might add that the very *names* by which Christians were known bear the same witness. That Christians were named Christians at all bears witness to their basic association with Jesus as Christ. It appears to have been a derisive term applied to them by unbelievers. Similarly, they were called the Nazarenes —a more obscure title, but again one which seems to point to their one distinctive tenet in their connexion with Jesus.[27] Their own terms for themselves were 'God's dedicated ones'—οἱ ἅγιοι—a term indicating their belief that Jesus was the embodiment of pious Israelites' hopes[28]; οἱ ἐν Χριστῷ, 'those who

[25] See Appendix I; also M. Hooker, *Jesus and the Servant*, 1959.
[26] Obvious examples are Mark 10.45 (Matt. 20.28), Mark 14.24 (Matt. 26.28); Rom. 3.25, 4.25, 5.6, 19, 8.3; I Cor. 1.18, 23 f.; II Cor. 5.21; Gal. 2.20; Eph. 2.14; Phil. 3.10; Col. 1.20; Heb. 10.9 f.; I Peter 2.24; I John 1.7, 2.2, 4.9 f.; Rev. 1.5.
[27] Despite various other theories (e.g. B. Gärtner, *Die rätselhaften Termini Nazoräer und Iskariot* [*Horae Soederblomianiae*, IV, 1957]; E. Schweizer, ' "Er wird Nazoräer heissen" [zu Mk 1.24, Mt 2.23]' in *Judentum, Urchristentum, Kirche* [Festschrift für J. Jeremias], Beiheft 26 zur *ZNW*, 1960; O. Cullmann, article 'Nazarene' in *The Interpreter's Dictionary* of the Bible), H. H. Schaeder, *TDNT* iv, 877, seems to have made a good case for its most obvious topographical meaning.
[28] The Hebrew or Aramaic equivalent—*ḥaqqᵉdôšîm* or *qaddîšîn*—is extremely rare in the Old Testament as a noun denoting human persons. See Deut. 33.3; Dan. 7.21 f., 8.24; Pss. 16.3, 34.9. Persons are frequently called

are incorporated in Christ'—an indication (as we shall see) of the new relationship mediated by Jesus; 'believers', οἱ πιστεύοντες or πιστοί, again, an index of the essentially declaratory nature of the Christian *differentia*. One other term, 'the way', ἡ ὁδός, might seem at first to afford grounds for estimating them as merely ethical teachers or moralists; but the 'way' in question, if one interrogates the New Testament itself, is the way of repentance, baptism, and faith—a religious way, not a new philosophy or ideology or ethic: a religious way mediated by Jesus. N. A. Dahl[29] was right when he said that the Christians had no new *halachah* (i.e. ethical teaching).

Conclusions

Thus, all the evidence converges on the conclusion—so far as I can see—that there was nothing to discriminate Christians initially from any other Jews of their day except their convictions about Jesus; and that it was these which kept them from lapsing back into Judaism, or, rather, which ultimately forced them out of Judaism; which means either that these convictions were justified or else, if they were not, that the rise and continuance of the Christian Church still await explanation. As an historical phenomenon, the coming into existence of the sect of the Nazarenes cannot be *explained* (it seems to me) by anything except its distinctive features: and these are due, if not to a huge reality, then to deliberate lying, or to misapprehension; and neither of these latter circumstances seems adequately to account for the facts.

What I have been anxious to do in this chapter is to see whether the argument from the existence of the Church to the rightness of the Christian estimate of Christ can be stated in such a way as to make it proof against the obvious attack—namely, that the mere existence of a body proves nothing as to the correctness of its tenets. I have asserted that this particular body had nothing to account for it except what it claimed about Jesus; and that all the

---

'holy' or told to become 'holy'; but the use of the word as a noun ('holy one') is mostly confined, in its application, to angels. See Ps. 89.6, 8; Job 5.1, 15.5; Zech. 14.5; Dan. 4.10, 14, 20, 8.13. When, therefore, it is used in this nominal way of persons, it presumably reflects the consciousness of Israelite sectarianism. The Christians wanted to be 'true Israel'. It was their distinctive conviction about Jesus that made Israel thrust them out.

[29] *Das Volk Gottes*, 161.

suggested explanations of those claims, other than the Christians'
own explanations, break down somewhere.

Equally clear is the fact that what the Christians alleged of
Jesus is something which cannot be confined within historical
terms. It transcends history; but, for all that, it is rooted in
history. It is rooted in history and is something to which eye-
witness is borne—appeal to eyewitness being an essential part of
the early Gospel.[30] Although it cannot be formulated without
the use of 'trans-historical' terms, yet the historical terms are also
essential; and, moreover, the New Testament writers know the
difference between the two.[31] To agree that the Christian estimate
of Jesus is in transcendent terms is not the same thing as saying
that there was, in history, nothing but the death of Jesus to
suggest the transcendent terms. Rather, it points to a decisive
event, in addition to the death, which can only be described as the
resurrection.[32]

[30] O. Cullmann, *Heil als Geschichte*, 1965, 81 (ET, *Salvation in History*, 1967).
[31] O. Cullmann, *ibid.*, 77, 83.
[32] See G. E. Ladd, *Jesus and the Kingdom*, 188, n. 2; V. Taylor, *The Person of Christ*, 1958, 186; W. Künneth, *The Theology of the Resurrection*, 249, 253.

II

THE CORPORATE CHRIST

THE thesis of Chapter I was that the beginnings of Christianity cannot be satisfactorily accounted for by any theory that does not recognize that the Christian community possessed nothing distinctive except the conviction that Jesus had been raised from among the dead—that the one who Jesus was had been raised to life absolute. The origin and rise of other movements may be explained, it was argued, by factors which anyone can recognize as valid, even if their peculiarities are discounted as invalid. But if the basic Christian conviction is discounted, it is difficult to know where else to look for an explosion powerful enough to launch the missile.

So, of the New Testament phenomena which are to be submitted to the historian, the first was the New Testament itself, as a whole, bearing witness to the coming into existence of the Church and its one basic conviction. And the question was, How do you explain this, on any postulate other than the Christian postulate? The second phenomenon, to which we now turn, is the extraordinary conception of the Lord Jesus Christ as a corporate, a more-than-individual personality.

In an attempt such as this to meet popular scepticism about the Christian estimate of Christ, it might seem strange to concentrate a whole chapter on the phrase 'in Christ' and ideas related to it. This formula is, no doubt, popularly supposed, by those who have ever heard of it at all, to be an index of the subjective piety of Paul and to belong to an esoteric mysticism far removed from anything that might seem to possess value as objective evidence of the authenticity of the Christian claim. In fact, however, I believe that it is a symptom of a stubborn fact which the historian needs to take account of—the fact, namely, that Christians from the beginning found themselves driven to an estimate of Jesus in more than merely individual terms. In this chapter, therefore,

21

I propose first to attempt a sketch of the significance of the term 'in Christ' (and related formulae) in the thinking of Paul: then to show that the estimate of Jesus which it implies was entertained, at least by implication, by other early Christians besides Paul: and finally, to ask whether the implications of such an estimate, as held by monotheistic Jews, do not constitute a most remarkable piece of evidence about Christian origins.

I. *'In Christ' and related phrases in Paul*

The literature on this term—from the celebrated monograph by Adolf Deissmann (1892) to the present day—is vast, and the theme is decidedly complicated. I must not attempt here to sketch in any detail the findings even of the more recent writers such as F. Büchsel, A. Oepke, E. Best, F. Neugebauer, and M. Bouttier.[1] But in brief it can be said that, if one starts by simply counting New Testament occurrences of ἐν followed by a designation of Jesus (e.g. Christ, the Lord, Christ Jesus), the vast preponderance is in the Pauline epistles. Elsewhere it is much less frequent, and does not occur at all in Hebrews, James, II Peter, or Jude.

But if one goes on to ask how often it clearly refers to *incorporation in Christ*, the number, even in the Paulines, is considerably reduced. Sometimes—if one is, for the moment, trying to minimize—it *need* only be an ἐν of instrument or agent. Thus: 'Sanctified *by* Christ Jesus' (ἡγιασμένοις ἐν X. 'I., I Cor. 1.2); 'God was reconciling the world to himself through Christ' (Θεὸς ἦν ἐν X. κόσμον καταλλάσσων ἑαυτῷ, II Cor. 5.19: but, in any case, this instance, with *God* as subject, falls outside our present concern); 'seeking to be justified *by* Christ' (ζητοῦντες δικαιωθῆναι ἐν X., Gal. 2.17). Or, relating not directly to persons but to things, it may be the almost literal ἐν of location: 'the love of God which is in Christ Jesus our Lord' (. . . τῆς ἀγάπης τοῦ Θεοῦ τῆς ἐν X. 'I. τῷ K. ἡμῶν, Rom. 8.39). Or, again, it may indicate the ground of authority: 'I am convinced *on the authority of* the Lord Jesus' (πέπεισμαι ἐν K. 'I., Rom. 14.14)[2]; 'we entreat you *on the authority of* the Lord Jesus'

---

[1] F. Büchsel, ' "In Christus" bei Paulus', *ZNW*, 42, 1949, 141 ff.; A. Oepke, *TDNT* ii, 541–3; E. Best, *One Body in Christ,* 1955; F. Neugebauer, 'Das paulinische "in Christo" ', *NTS*, 4.2, 1958, 124 ff.; *id., In Christus, Untersuchung zum paulinischen Glaubensverständnis,* 1961; M. Bouttier, *En Christ,* 1962.

[2] The late Fr Gabriel Hebert, in a letter, suggested that this might be a reference to the saying of Jesus in Mark 7.14 ff.

(παρακαλοῦμεν ἐν K. ’I., I Thess. 4.1, cf. v. 2, διὰ τοῦ K. ’I.,
v. 15, ἐν λόγῳ Κυρίου).

I do not hold that these renderings are all correct, or that the
categories are thus correctly defined. They are merely cited as
examples of uses of ἐν which *need* not be incorporative, if one is
trying to minimize the category.

Very often, again, it appears to denote a hard-to-define relationship—something, perhaps, as vague as 'in the Christian
sphere'. It may be that, in the end, many of these will turn out to
belong in the properly incorporative category, or in other clearly
defined classes; but, for the time being, they ought to be counted
out. Examples (quite arbitrarily selected) are: 'I have, then,
something to boast of in the Lord Jesus' (ἔχω οὖν τὴν καύχησιν
ἐν K. ’I., Rom. 15.17); 'welcome [her] in the Lord' (προσδέξησθε
ἐν K., Rom. 16.2); 'give my greetings . . . in Christ Jesus'
(ἀσπάσασθε . . . ἐν X. ’I., Rom. 16.3); 'I was glad . . . in the
Lord' (ἐχάρην . . . ἐν K., Phil. 4.10). The NEB rendering, in
some of these instances, comes down on the more definitely
incorporative side, but the rough renderings just offered here are
sufficient indication of the vagueness of such phrases. Comparable,
perhaps, is what C. H. Dodd calls 'the usage of the LXX where
such expressions as "rejoice in the Lord", "in the Lord is ever-
lasting strength", leave the particular connotation of the preposi-
tion quite vague'.[3] But, all allowance made—and as has been
said, some of the above examples might need to be brought out
of this doubtful category into something more definite—there is
at the least a residuum of occurrences where it unmistakably
describes *the incorporation of believers in Christ*.

Examples of this clearly incorporative use are the following.
First there are such phrases as 'those who are in Christ Jesus' (e.g.,
Rom. 8.1—'there is no condemnation for those who are united
with Christ Jesus'—NEB). Then, the striking words of Rom.
16.7, '. . . who . . . came to be in Christ' (οἳ . . . γέγοναν ἐν
Χριστῷ—NEB, 'they were Christians'). Still more decisive is
the parallel, in I Cor. 15.22, between being 'in Adam'—that is,
incorporated in humanity, part of the human race—and being
'in Christ'. Finally—to go no further—there is Phil. 3.8 f., where
Paul says that his ambition is to be found to be in Christ (ἵνα . . .

---

[3] *The Interpretation of the Fourth Gospel*, 1953, 192.

εὑρεθῶ ἐν αὐτῷ—'finding myself incorporate in him'—NEB).[4]

It is clear enough that at least this group of occurrences—if not many other less clearly definable uses of ἐν—reflects a conviction that Christ is an *inclusive personality*.

It is perfectly true, of course, that occasionally Christ is spoken of as, conversely, in the believer. If the instances were equally balanced in either direction—Paul in Christ, and Christ in Paul—we might be inclined to explain the ἐν Χριστῷ of Paul as indicating not a corporate personality but simply one side of the mutual interpenetration of two individuals in intimate relationship.[5] This, as we shall see, is the probable meaning of the Johannine usage of this ἐν. But in Paul the 'Christ in us' formula is decidedly rare. We may at once discount two instances where it probably means not 'in' but 'among': II Cor. 13.5, NEB, 'Jesus Christ is among you'; Col. 1.27, NEB margin, 'Christ is among you'. A third, Gal. 4.19, is ambiguous: μέχρις οὗ μορφωθῇ X. ἐν ὑμῖν (NEB 'until you take the shape of Christ'; but is it 'you' collectively, or 'each of you'?). And another, Col. 3.11 (NEB, 'Christ is all, and is in all', πάντα καὶ ἐν πᾶσιν X.) is perhaps, despite the NEB rendering, a mere 'superlative' ('all in all', 'absolutely everything'), and not to be pressed in detail. What remains, then, is Rom. 8.10, 'if Christ is dwelling in you . . .' (a fairly clear instance); and a series of ἐν-phrases with Christ as subject, all combined with verbs other than the verb to be. This latter use perhaps means that, while Paul could freely speak of the Christian not only living and acting but actually being and existing

---

[4] Sometimes the verb 'to be' is implied, as in Rom. 8.1 (and *passim*), Rom. 16.7, and I Cor. 15.22 (all just quoted); I Cor. 15.18 ('those who have fallen asleep in Christ' = 'those who fell asleep *while being* in Christ', οἱ κοιμηθέντες ἐν X.); II Cor. 5.17 ('if anyone [comes to be] in Christ', εἴ τις ἐν X.); II Cor. 12.2 ('I know a man [who was] in Christ', οἶδα ἄνθρωπον ἐν X.); Phil. 3.8 f. (just quoted). Examples of other words—words denoting activities exercised by Christians as incorporate in Christ—may conveniently be drawn from Rom. 16: v. 9 ('Urbanus, our fellow-worker, συνεργόν, in Christ'), v. 12 ('Tryphaena and Tryphosa who toil in the Lord', τὰς κοπιώσας ἐν K., . . . my dear Persis, who has toiled much in the Lord, πολλὰ ἐκοπίασεν ἐν K.), etc., etc. I would *not* include—despite a prevailing fashion among commentators—Phil. 2.5, where the NEB text renders: 'Let your bearing towards one another arise out of your life in Christ Jesus.' I would favour the margin: 'Have this bearing towards one another which was also found in Christ Jesus.' Cf. E. Larsson, *Christus als Vorbild*, 1962, 232 f.

[5] Cf., perhaps, Phil. 1.7, 'because you hold me in such affection' (literally, '. . . have me in the heart', διὰ τὸ ἔχειν με ἐν τῇ καρδίᾳ ὑμᾶς).

'in the sphere of Christ' (though often with the verb 'to be' *implied* rather than stated), when it came to the converse—Christ in us—he tended to think not of Christ incorporate in the believer but rather of Christ 'at work', or 'living his life' in the believers. But there are undeniably a few notable exceptions. Eph. 3.17 is certainly very striking: 'that through faith Christ may dwell in your hearts', κατοικῆσαι τὸν Χ. διὰ τῆς πίστεως ἐν ταῖς καρδίαις ὑμῶν. 'Dwelling in your hearts' is, of course, much the same as 'being in you', . . . ἐν ὑμῖν, and is undeniably individual. And Gal. 2.20 is, admittedly, a signal and most remarkably reciprocal phrase: 'the life which Christ lives in me', . . . ζῇ δὲ ἐν ἐμοὶ Χ., is tantamount to 'Christ is in me'. But apart from these, there is a strong tendency to speak in terms only of Christ's *activity*, rather than *existence*, in us. Even here, many of the phrases may better be rendered by 'among' rather than 'within' (as, clearly, Gal. 3.5, '. . . works miracles among you', ὁ . . . ἐνεργῶν δυνάμεις ἐν ὑμῖν); but some at least of the following will serve as examples despite the NEB deciding otherwise in some cases:

I Cor. 12.6 (where it is not even *Christ*, but *God*!), 'all of them, in all men, are the work of the same God', . . . Θεὸς ὁ ἐνεργῶν τὰ πάντα ἐν πᾶσιν.

II Cor. 13.3, 'the Christ who speaks through me', . . . τοῦ ἐν ἐμοὶ λαλοῦντος Χ.

Gal. 2.8, 'God whose action made Peter an apostle to the Jews, also made me an apostle to the Gentiles' (literally 'worked in Peter . . . in me'), ὁ γὰρ ἐνεργήσας Πέτρῳ . . . ἐνήργησεν καὶ ἐμοί.

Eph. 3.20, 'by the power which is at work among us', κατὰ τὴν δύναμιν τὴν ἐνεργουμένην ἐν ἡμῖν.

Phil. 2.13 (again *God*, not *Christ*), 'for it is God who works in you, inspiring both the will . . .', Θεὸς γάρ ἐστιν ὁ ἐνεργῶν ἐν ὑμῖν καὶ τὸ θέλειν . . .

Col. 1.29, 'with all the energy and power of Christ at work in me', κατὰ τὴν ἐνέργειαν αὐτοῦ τὴν ἐνεργουμένην ἐν ἐμοὶ . . .

Col. 3.16, 'let the message of Christ dwell among you . . .', ὁ λόγος τοῦ Χριστοῦ ἐνοικείτω ἐν ὑμῖν . . .

Thus, the terms are, admittedly, in some measure correlative and reciprocal: as Christians exercise their activities in Christ, so God and Christ are at work in Christians. But—and here is the difference—in the 'we in Christ' formula Christians are thought of (by implication as we have seen) as having their very location, their very existence and status, in Christ; whereas Christ is *not*—or only very seldom—spoken of correlatively as thus existing in Christians.

Even more significant, I think, is Dr Best's observation[6] that even if the whole Christ dwells in each believer, 'it is the corporate whole of believers who dwell in Christ': it is most emphatically, therefore, not the mere mutual interpenetration of two individuals.

It is a striking observation of M. Bouttier's[7] that, broadly speaking, the reverse holds for the Pauline phrases with the Spirit: the idea of the Spirit as being in Christians is a more fundamental idea than that of Christians as being in the Spirit. It is still more striking that certain subtle differences may be detected in the ἐν-phrases as between the use of Χριστός and Κύριος. Very roughly speaking and without complete consistency,[8] the Χριστός-phrases tend to be indicative, 'kerygmatic' statements, relating to the work of God and to what, in Christ, Christians *are*; the Κύριος-phrases tend to be imperative, ethical exhortations, urging Christians to *become* what they are.[9] The formulae could be summed up and combined as 'Become, *in the Lord*, what you already are *in Christ*!'

All this, I think, adds up to, not a proof but at least a strong indication, that although Paul viewed the Lord Jesus Christ as one who had indeed direct relations with each individual Christian, he did not view him as a mere individual, but rather as an inclusive personality: one in whom Christians are incorporated by

---

[6] *One Body in Christ*, 9.   [7] *En Christ*, 84, n. 65.

[8] It would, for instance, be extremely difficult to find an entirely rational explanation for all the fluctuations within Rom. 16.

[9] See Neugebauer and Bouttier *passim*, and also W. Kramer, *Christ, Lord, Son of God* (ET, SBT 50, 1966, of the 1963 German edition). Also F. Gerritzen, O.S.B., 'Le Sens et l'origine de l'*EN ΧΡΙΣΤΩΙ* paulinien', in *Analecta Biblica*, 1963, ii, 323 ff. Examples are: (*a*) *In Christ*: 'in Christ Jesus you are my offspring, and mine alone, through the preaching of the Gospel' (ἐν γὰρ Χ. Ἰ. διὰ τοῦ εὐαγγελίου ἐγὼ ὑμᾶς ἐγέννησα), I Cor. 4.15. (*b*) *In the Lord*: 'I beg Euodia, and I beg Syntyche, to agree together in the Lord's fellowship' (Εὐ. παρακαλῶ καὶ Σ. παρακαλῶ τὸ αὐτὸ φρονεῖν ἐν Κ.), Phil. 4.2. A rather striking fusion of the 'kerygmatic' and the ethical seems to be provided by Col. 2.6: 'Therefore, since Jesus was delivered to you as Christ and Lord, live your lives in union with him' (ὡς οὖν παρελάβετε τὸν Χριστὸν Ἰησοῦν τὸν Κύριον, ἐν αὐτῷ περιπατεῖτε).

baptism. Dr Best writes: '. . . the formula "in Christ" contains two fundamental ideas: believers are in Christ; salvation is in Christ. In both the ἐν is taken at its full value. Sometimes one idea predominates and sometimes the other; they are held together by the conception of Christ as a corporate personality. . . .'[10] That this is not thought of in quasi-material terms—as though of immersing in some fluid—is clear, if only because of the personal language consistently adopted.[11] That it is not a *union of identity* is equally clear, because of the strong sense of individual choice and responsibility, of dialogue with Christ, and of personal friendship, that pervades Paul's thought.[12] But that it is an organic relationship is not only suggested by these phrases but confirmed by Paul's celebrated language about the body and the limbs, and by his wealth of compounds with σύν.

For completeness' sake, we may add, before turning to these usages, that he also speaks, though far less frequently, of Christians being incorporated in God. Probably this only occurs twice (I Thess. 1.1 and II Thess. 1.1) for the other candidates are hardly comparable: 'hidden with Christ in God', Col. 3.3; '[the mystery] was hidden in God', Eph. 3.9; 'by the help of our God' (i.e. the NEB takes ἐν to be of agent), I Thess. 2.2; 'You are proud of your God', Rom. 2.17; 'we also exult in God', Rom. 5.11. The last two are ways of expressing that God himself is the ground or object of exultation. E. Best[13] observes that the two main 'in God' phrases are in the early, Thessalonian epistles: Paul perhaps later found it difficult to say that men are 'in God', and he therefore retained and elaborated the 'in Christ' formula. Paul does not ever speak, as John does, of Christ being in God (even Col. 3.3 does not quite say this).

In view, then, of the significant uses of ἐν in the Pauline epistles, it is probable, as C. H. Dodd[14] remarks, that Schweitzer was right in seeing Paul's use of ἐν as equivalent to his idea of the limbs in the body. It is a genuinely incorporative idea. At any rate the figure of the Body furnishes another line of evidence; and so does the figure of the Temple. The idea of Christ as the Body

---

[10] *One Body in Christ*, 29.
[11] See F. C. Porter, *The Mind of Christ in Paul*, 1932.
[12] See A. R. George, *Communion with God in the New Testament*, 1953.
[13] *One Body in Christ*, 22.
[14] C. H. Dodd, *The Interpretation of the Fourth Gospel*, 1953, 193.

of which Christians are parts has been widely commented on, and need not be elaborated here.[15] The Temple-figure has not received so much attention in published works. It is noteworthy that, whereas the Qumran community thought of themselves collectively as the Temple, there seems to be no sign of their applying this terminology to any of their individual messianic figures.[16] In contrast, the New Testament epistles apply the Temple language to the community *as bonded together by Christ* or *growing together round Christ* (Eph. 2.21 f.; I Peter 2.4 f.). The Temple-figure comes also, without explicit mention of Christ, in I Cor. 3.16; but only a few verses earlier, Christ is the 'foundation' (v. 11). And St John's Gospel, despite any individualism we may detect when we come, directly, to its use of $\dot{\varepsilon}\nu$, actually interprets the Temple in terms of Christ's Body (John 2.21). Thus, Paul, supplemented in this latter respect by John, is ready to speak of Christ not only as the Body in which Christians belong as limbs and organs, but also as at least the essential part of the Temple which they constitute.

If we continue, for a moment, to consider Pauline usage, it is

[15] See, e.g., J. A. T. Robinson, *The Body: a Study in Pauline Theology*, SBT 5, 1952.
[16] See B. Gärtner, *The Temple and Community in Qumran and the New Testament*, 1965. An important example of the building-metaphor in the thought of the Qumran sect is 1QS 8.5–9:
[5]the council of the community will be established in truth for an eternal planting, a house of holiness for Israel, a company of holy [6]of holies for Aaron, witnesses to truth for the judgment and chosen by good will to atone for the land and to requite [7]the wicked with their reward. It shall be a trusty wall, a precious cornerstone: their foundations will not [8]shift nor shall they move from their places. A dwelling which is a holy of holies [9]for Aaron in the knowledge of all, for a covenant of justice and to offer a pleasant savour, and a perfect house and truth in Israel. . . . (A. R. C. Leaney's version, in *The Rule of Qumran and its Meaning*, 1966, 209).
Cf. 1QS 5.5 f.:
[5]. . . he shall . . . lay a foundation of truth for Israel to make a community of an eternal covenant; [6]make atonement for all who offer themselves to holiness in Aaron or to the house of truth in Israel . . . (*id.*, 161); and 9.5 f.: [5]. . . at that time the men [6]of the community shall separate themselves as a house of holiness for Aaron and to be united as a holy of holies, and as a house of holiness for Israel who walk in perfection (*id.*, 210).
Isa. 28.16 ('Behold I am laying in Zion for a foundation a stone, a tested stone, a precious cornerstone, of a sure foundation . . .') is clearly in view in such passages.
All this is discussed by R. J. McKelvey in an unpublished thesis. It shows that the notion of a community as a temple did exist on Palestinian soil in New Testament times independently of the Christian movement; but it seems also to point to the difference between the two, and to the distinctiveness of Christian thought.

worth noting that the idea of Christ's death being salvific for others is itself a further indication of a more than individual conception of his person. An individual may lay down his life in an attempt, successful or unsuccessful, to rescue someone else, or even a plurality of other persons; but it is difficult to see how an individual's death could somehow be a source of release from evil and of new life 'for many'. 'Was it Paul who was crucified for you?' exclaims Paul indignantly, when the Corinthians are indulging in personality cults (I Cor. 1.13). Similarly, the idea in Rom. 5.19 of the one man's obedience being valid for the many is hard not to place in the same corporate realm as the ἐν Χριστῷ formula, especially when the parallel is so inclusive a figure as Adam. Indeed, there is no passage in Paul's writings that shows more clearly than Rom. 5.12–19 that, in such a connexion, Paul could think of Christ in the same way as he thought of Adam, as the inclusive personality of the whole race. Adam and Christ are alike in this, that their actions were representative and inclusive. In this respect, Adam is a 'type' (τύπος) of the Man who was to come (v. 14). It is in keeping with this that M. Bouttier derives the sayings of Paul about suffering and dying *with* Christ (σὺν Χριστῷ) from the formula 'on our behalf' (ὑπὲρ ἡμῶν). σὺν Χριστῷ, Bouttier says, is extracted from ὑπὲρ ἡμῶν like gold from the ore: if Christ lived, died, and was raised *for us*, then he recapitulates our needs.[17] There is a wealth of words compounded with σύν, 'together with', which bear out this consciousness, e.g.: συζῆν, 'to have life with' (Rom. 6.8); συμμορφίζεσθαι, 'to be conformed with' (Phil. 3.10); σύμμορφος, 'conformed with' (Rom. 8.29; Phil. 3.21); συμπάσχειν, 'to suffer with' (Rom. 8.17); σύμφυτος, 'grown together with' (Rom. 6.5); συνδοξά- ζεσθαι, 'to be glorified with' (Rom. 8.17); συνθάπτεσθαι, 'to be buried with' (Rom. 6.4); συσταυροῦσθαι, 'to be crucified with' (Rom. 6.6; Gal. 2.19). It is, of course, the context that often determines a meaning relevant to this argument. 'To be crucified with' is also used, though not with the compound verb, of mere simultaneity, in Mark 15.27; Matt. 27.38.

II. *Outside the Pauline Epistles*

So much, then, for the evidence in Paul of a supra-individual estimate of Christ. But is not this only an abnormality—the

[17] *En Christ*, 45.

eccentric thinking of a very exceptional Christian? A mysteriously corporate notion of the person of Christ evidenced by Paul alone would scarcely, however remarkable, constitute evidence that such an estimate was part of the common convictions of primitive Christianity and therefore an authentic pointer to an experience of Jesus of Nazareth as more than a merely individual, human personality.

In reply to this question, it seems to me that, although it is true that not all New Testament writers evince the same explicit awareness as Paul, yet the same estimate of Jesus is implied by hints elsewhere also. There is no denying that although some of the other writers (as we shall see) do seem to regard Jesus as exalted and more than human, yet it is as an exalted and more than human individual rather than the inclusive personality indicated by Paul. And this seems to be true of John. He differs from Paul in his use of ἐν in at least two respects. First, behind the relationship between Christ and his disciples lies, according to the Johannine conception, a comparable relation between Christ and God. As C. H. Dodd remarks,[18] it is essential to the Johannine position 'that the relation ἐγὼ ἐν τῷ πατρὶ καὶ ὁ πατὴρ ἐν ἐμοί ['I in the Father and the Father in me'] (see 14.11; 17.21) is the direct archetype of the relation ὑμεῖς ἐν ἐμοὶ κἀγὼ ἐν ὑμῖν ['you in me and I in you'].' This is something which, as we have seen, Paul does not make explicit. Even Col. 3.3 (if that is Pauline—as I am ready to believe it is) is not exactly like the Johannine conception. But for John it is basic. John 17.21–23 will suffice as an illustration:

. . . may they all be one; as thou, Father, art in me, and I in thee, so also may they be in us, that the world may believe that thou didst send me. The glory which thou gavest me I have given to them, that they may be one, as we are one; I in them and thou in me, may they be perfectly one. . . .

But more important for our purposes is a second difference—an indication of individualism in John. The most obvious parallel to the ἐν Χριστῷ of Paul might, at first sight, seem to be in the Johannine writings, where there is a striking use of ἐν. In particular, the analogy of the vine and its branches in John 15 seems, at first, to present a good parallel to the Pauline analogy

---

[18] *The Interpretation of the Fourth Gospel*, 193.

of the body and its limbs, and John 15.4^b, if it were isolated from its context, could very easily be thought to express the Pauline idea: '. . . as the branch cannot bear fruit of itself unless it remains in the vine, so neither can you, unless you remain in me'. But further reflexion shows that, for John, the relationship is re-ciprocal—Christ in us, as much as we in Christ, whereas this is precisely what we have noticed does not obtain for Paul. The opening phrase of the very verse just quoted provides an example of the completely reciprocal relationship intended by John: 'Remain in me, and I [will remain] in you' (John 15.4^a). And this absolutely reciprocal relationship is instanced elsewhere also in John 15.5: 'Whoever remains in me and I in him, he bears much fruit.'

Now in all this, as it seems to me, there is an individualism which distinguishes it from Paul's way of thinking. The ἐν-formula, both as applied to the relation between Jesus and God and as applied to that between Jesus and his disciples, is con-sistently used in both directions—I in him and he in me—in such a way as to show that the model (so to speak) on which it is fashioned is simply the mutual interpenetration of two individual persons. There is in John none of the Pauline preponderance of the use of the phrase in the one direction—we in Christ.[19]

On the other hand, there are hints in John which restore the balance. It is clear enough that, for John, what is meant by the disciples 'abiding' in Christ is that they trust in him and obey his commands. John uses μένειν, 'abide', in a characteristic way, both of Christ's abiding in his Father and of the disciples abiding in Christ; and, in both cases, it is interpreted in terms of obedience.

This being so, although it is true that Christ, reciprocally, is spoken of as 'abiding' in the disciples, it is obvious that there is no question of his obeying them. Correspondingly, even if the vine is very nearly spoken of, paradoxically, as abiding in the branches (John 15.5), the image makes it obvious enough that, in fact, the relationship cannot be precisely the same in both directions: the vine cannot actually abide in a branch in the same sense as that in which the branch can in the vine.

Thus, although the Johannine ἐν by itself reflects a more indivi-dualistic conception of Christ's person, and although, as I believe,

[19] Note, incidentally, that even here, there is nothing of the union of identity which meets us in some other religions.

the Fourth Evangelist evinces this tendency in other ways also,[20] it is used in contexts which, despite this, reflect the sense of Christ's inclusiveness. The figure of the Temple, applied to Christ's body (John 2.21) has already been alluded to. This again, suggests that it is in Christ that man worships the Father. In other words, the Fourth Evangelist is bearing witness almost, as it were, despite himself, to the difficulty of confining Christ to an individual model.

But, once again, Paul and John are, on any showing, giants of religious genius. Are we not still far from establishing that this conception of Christ as an inclusive personality was something compelling in early Christianity generally? One more outstanding writer must first be summoned in evidence, the writer of the Epistle to the Hebrews. In the main, his attitude to Christian allegiance might be described as far more external, far less 'mystical', than either Paul's or John's. This writer thinks of Christian allegiance as heroic faith—faith in the unseen values, the courage to step out upon the unknown, the daring of ardent loyalty which follows Christ as a soldier follows the leader he believes in. The relationship between Christ and Christian, according to the Epistle to the Hebrews, is more often in such terms as these than in terms of the organic union of body and limbs or vine and branches.

Yet even here there are exceptions, and they are the more arresting because they intrude despite the prevailingly different tone. The most notable of these is the use of Ps. 8 in Heb. 2.6 ff.:

But there is somewhere a solemn assurance which runs:

'What is man, that thou rememberest him,
Or the son of man, that thou hast regard to him?
Thou didst make him for a short while lower than the angels;
Thou didst crown him with glory and honour;
Thou didst put all things in subjection beneath his feet.'

For in subjecting all things to him, he left nothing that is not subject.

It seems best to take 'man' (*ᵉnôš*) and 'the son of man' (*ben-âdâm*) in Ps. 8, here quoted, as intended by the writer to the Hebrews to mean Humanity; and then to interpret what follows the quotation to mean that, whereas Humanity collectively has

[20] See my paper: 'The Individualism of the Fourth Gospel', *NovTest*, v, 1962, 171 ff.

fallen dismally short of the ideal—the 'glory'—described as God's intention for him in the Psalms, we do see *in Jesus* the realization of the ideal; and its realization, moreover, inclusively and on behalf of the rest of mankind: vv. 8ᵇ f.:

> But in fact we do not yet see all things in subjection to man. In Jesus, however, we do see one who for a short while was made lower than the angels, crowned now with glory and honour because he suffered death, so that, by God's gracious will, in tasting death he should stand for us all.

This means that we are presented here with a doctrine of Christ as the Second (or rather the Last or Ultimate) Adam comparable to Paul's in Rom. 5 or I Cor. 15, though apparently quite independent of it, and, indeed, of the writer's own tendencies—an essentially *corporate* and *inclusive* conception of Christ.

Similar to this, I think it may justly be argued, is the reasoning of chapter 10. Here, as is well known, the writer employs a perhaps mistaken reading of the Greek Bible for his own purposes. He cites Ps. 40 in the form '. . . a *body* hast thou prepared . . .'; and proceeds to relate this to the self-surrender of Christ in an act of total and perfect obedience to the will of God. And then (verse 10)—'by this will we have been sanctified': that is, Christ's act of obedience is as inclusive as Paul shows it to be when he says in Rom. 5 that a single act of obedience meant a putting right of all mankind, or when he says in II Cor. 5 that if one died for all, then all were dead. Even in Hebrews, then, despite its generally different emphasis, a doctrine of the inclusiveness of Christ from time to time asserts itself.

But even now, we have the evidence only of the outstanding religious figures, not of the rank and file. Even if the three strands of thought we have examined (Paul, John, Hebrews) are independent and constitute a genuinely cumulative witness, it might still be argued that they do not provide compelling evidence for the nature of Jesus himself, but only reflect the inventions of religious aspiration. What, then, we must now ask, of the remaining evidence? As a matter of fact, it is very considerable.

The Synoptic Gospels are not specially primitive in date, as compared with the Pauline epistles, but neither do they purport to be representative of the religious aspirations of their writers. Rather, they are, I believe, an attempt to explain Christian origins —not to mention the genuinely primitive traditions which they, in part, preserve. And one important piece of evidence seems to me to emerge from them—that 'the Son of Man' was a term used by Jesus. Practically all critics discount some of 'the Son of Man' sayings as later, unauthentic additions. Some critics would deny that Jesus himself used the term at all. Many would deny that, even if Jesus did use the term, he meant to indicate himself thereby. Others, allowing that he meant himself, hold that the term had nothing to do with Daniel's vision (Dan. 7) or with any symbolic figure, but was merely a circumlocution for 'that man' or 'myself'. It would be quite impossible here to discuss the evidence.[21] I can only say that, after many years of pondering, I find myself more and more convinced by the view that derives the term primarily from Dan. 7, where 'the human figure' is a symbol for the martyr-group of loyal Jews coming through persecution and vindicated by God; that I believe it is most natural (without denying that some of the uses in the Gospels are later) to take it as Jesus' chosen self-designation; and that, if so, it

---

[21] For the relevant books and articles, see lists in A. J. B. Higgins, *Jesus and the Son of Man*, 1964, and H. E. Tödt, *The Son of Man in the Synoptic Tradition*, ET, 1965, of *der Menschensohn in der synoptischen Überlieferung*[2], 1963. Both authors think that there are some genuinely dominical uses, but that in none of these did Jesus apply the term to himself. The main factor dividing my own view, which is substantially that of some other British writers, from the view of many Continental scholars is my refusal to assume that an *individual, supernatural* 'Son of Man' was part of the mental furniture of Jesus himself or his contemporaries. In Dan. 8.15, the Angel Gabriel is described, in a Hebrew passage, as 'like a man' (*kᵉ marʾēh gāber*, in allusion, probably, to the name, Gabriel); but this is not quite the same. The only direct evidence so far available for the use of the term, 'the Son of Man', to connote such a figure comes from documents whose date is uncertain and of which it cannot be affirmed that they are pre-Christian. The relevant part of I Enoch is conspicuous for its absence from the copies of that book so far discovered at Qumran; and II Esdras 13, notoriously of uncertain date, was at any rate probably written after the death of Jesus and too late to be taken into account even in the early Church's shaping of traditions. The only relevant document that was certainly in existence early enough is Daniel 7; and, since Gospel traditions represent Jesus as alluding to it, the burden of proof would seem to rest on those who refuse to recognize it as the proximate source of his usage. Moreover, it makes good sense. In Dan. 7, the 'Son of Man' figure stands for the people of the saints of the Most High—evidently, that is, the martyr loyalists of Israel who suffer at the hands of Antiochus Epiphanes (Dan. 7.25) and are prepared to die sooner than surrender their faith. It is thus the ideal symbol for Christ's vocation, together with his associates. The strength of studies such as those of A. J. B. Higgins and H. E. Tödt is their careful analysis of sources, making a strong case for assigning different applications of 'the Son of Man' to different strata of

suggests (as T. W. Manson[22] consistently held) that Jesus interpreted his mission in terms of a corporate activity. This is consistent with the choice of the Twelve and the responsibilities committed to them: 'I tell you this: in the world that is to be, when the Son of Man is seated on his throne in heavenly splendour, you my followers will have thrones of your own, where you will sit as judges of the twelve tribes of Israel' (Matt. 19.28); 'You are the men who have stood firmly by me in my times of trial; and now I vest in you the kingship which my Father vested in me; you shall eat and drink at my table in my kingdom and sit on thrones as judges of the twelve tribes of Israel' (Luke 22.28–30). Admittedly, the Matthean passage, as it now stands, clearly distinguishes between the Son of Man and the Twelve; but that is quite easily explained, if Jesus, as the heart and centre of the corporate Son of Man, is himself, *par excellence*, called the Son of Man—whether by himself, if the saying is original, or by the Evangelist, if the saying has been modified. An awareness of the judicial function of the Christian community (comparable to that of the Son of Man) emerges also in I Cor. 6.3: 'Are you not aware that we are to judge angels? How much more, mere matters of business!'

This collective interpretation is widely questioned[23]; but I would appeal mainly to the coherence—as I see it—of the account which is yielded by it. It is well represented by the diagram of the converging lines which finally intersect and begin again to diverge. Jesus concentrates into himself all that man was originally meant to be in relation to God—he is, in that sense, the Son of Man. He

---

tradition. But strata of tradition may represent selection out of a single original collection, rather than being mutually exclusive; and there is no need to believe that the sayings in one stratum are exclusive of those in another unless the two are positively incompatible. There seems to me to be no *a priori* unlikelihood in the hypothesis that Jesus, having adopted the Danielic 'Son of Man' as a symbol for the martyr people destined to be vindicated through suffering, then applied it also to his own present circumstances. See my review of H. E. Tödt's book in *Theology*, lxix, 550 (April 1966), 172 ff. Miss M. Hooker's forthcoming monograph on the Son of Man in Mark (SPCK) deserves close attention. See, further, Appendix I, pp. 82 ff.

[22] E.g. *The Teaching of Jesus*, 1931; *The Servant-Messiah*, 1953.

[23] E.g. W. G. Kümmel calls it downright 'impossible' in *Promise and Fulfilment*, ET 1957, 66. See, however, a useful discussion in D. S. Russell, *The Method and Message of Jewish Apocalyptic*, 1964, reaching a conclusion (352) that the corporate interpretation has much to be said for it.

also perfectly exemplifies all that Daniel's 'Man' stood for when it represented the martyr-loyalists of the Maccabaean age. The lines converge on Jesus, who draws them into brilliant focus. But, equally, it is from him that the lines diverge again to include a company of people, as he draws into his vocation first his inner circle, the Twelve, and then, through them, the larger body.

Thus, at the point where the lines intersect is a figure into whom have been gathered and canalized all the converging streams of response to God. Or, looking at the diagram in another, but a complementary, light, here is the narrowing area of response to God, narrowing to a faithful remnant and, then, ultimately, to a single individual—but to an individual such that from his obedience even to death and extinction there broadens out also the area of a new responsiveness. If Jesus did use 'the Son of Man' to designate the responsive remnant, vindicated through martyrdom; if he did apply it to himself, as the focus and summary and recapitulation of that attitude; and if he was raised from among the dead and gathered into himself his followers, all this makes coherent the scattered evidences we have so far looked at.

Moreover, and this reminds us of evidence already adduced, it helps to explain the use of Scripture outside the Gospels also. I alluded, in my first chapter, to the unifying force of Christ in the co-ordinating of Scripture. Scriptures originally descriptive of ideal Israel or of Israel's representative leader are made to converge on Jesus; and the Christian use of Scripture is thus itself part of the evidence for the Christian estimate of Christ.

Further, there are to be taken into account such sayings as 'anything you did for one of my brothers here, however humble, you did for me' (Matt. 25.40, etc.)—an identification of Jesus with his own, which is reflected in the striking 'Saul, Saul, why do you persecute me?' of the Damascus road (Acts 9.4; 22.7; 26.14—all three versions).

About this, we must here digress for a little. One of the features which most emphatically distinguishes the Christology of Luke-Acts from that of Paul is precisely that Luke's Jesus remains individual. Luke's Gospel, like the other Synoptic Gospels, contains material such as those Son of Man sayings which, as I have just been arguing, imply a corporate idea. But he does not himself seem consciously to recognize the implication.

For his own part, Luke seems even more individualistic than (as I see it) John is. Even as the exalted Lord of the post-resurrection faith and of the apostolic preaching in the Acts, Jesus seems to remain, in Luke's imagination, an *individual* exalted Being. The chief grounds for saying this are the consistency with which, in the Acts, Jesus is represented as (so to speak) 'absent': he is seated at God's right hand in heaven, whence he has 'poured forth' the Holy Spirit. It is the Holy Spirit that, as it were, 'represents' Jesus' activity on earth and in the Christian mission. Jesus has gone up into heaven and will be there until he returns at the end. If he is seen at all by men, it is expressly in vision. Even the supreme encounter of the Damascus Road is with a Jesus who is a visitant *from heaven*. And, correspondingly, there is never a trace of an 'incorporative' awareness such as we have been examining in Paul and John and even Hebrews, unless the ἐν τῷ Ἰησοῦ of Acts 4.2 is to be so construed, which seems unlikely. The phrase, quite literally, is: 'to proclaim in Jesus the resurrection, the [resurrection] from the dead.' At the most, this phrase may mean that 'in Jesus' *the* resurrection, absolutely, has taken place—an idea which certainly might carry implications of a corporate Christology, but which hardly makes it explicit; and, if not, then it merely means 'in the case of Jesus'. The NEB renders it: '. . . the resurrection from the dead—the resurrection of Jesus'. Luke, it may be added, is the one Synoptist who does not include the saying about the Son of Man giving his life as a ransom for many. This saying, which comes in Mark and Matthew, is of the type already considered, which implies more than an individual's action. It is true that there are one or two comparable phrases in the accounts of the Maccabaean martyrs: I Macc. 6.44, Eleazar 'gave his life to save his people'; II Macc. 7.37 f., 'I, like my brothers, give up body and life for the laws of our fathers, appealing to God to show mercy soon to our nation . . . and through me and my brothers to bring to an end the wrath of the Almighty which has justly fallen on our whole nation'; IV Macc. 17.21: The result of Eleazar's martyrdom, with his companions, is that they became as it were a substitute (or satisfaction, ἀντίψυχον) for the nation's sin. But the ransom-saying in Mark 10.45 (Matt. 20.28), coupled with the institution of the Lord's Supper, is extremely difficult to interpret except in terms of inclusive personality.

But to return to Luke—if Luke is thus blind to this important incorporative aspect of Christology which we have found explicit in Paul, and if he has even eliminated other significant passages, it is all the more impressive that he should have retained, in his traditions both of the ministry of Jesus and of the Damascus Road, other parts of the raw material from which he might have made the deduction. The phrase 'Jesus, whom you are persecuting' occurs in all three accounts of the Damascus Road encounter (Acts 9.5; 22.8; 26.15), despite their variations in other respects. Luke seems here, and in his Gospel, to be reporting better than he understood—reporting phrases implying an incorporative, or, at the very least, representative, Christology such as is implied in the Gospels and is made explicit in the ἐν Χριστῷ and σῶμα language of the theologians.

Thus, Luke provides an instance of a phenomenon which is common enough at all periods, not least our own day. He is the devout Christian who uses the common stock of Christian traditions and ideas without necessarily being alive even to all their more obvious implications. But the fact that he retains the traditions only adds to the evidence for their weight and tenacity.

Here, then, even in the Synoptic Gospels and Acts are weighty considerations in favour of an inclusive interpretation of Jesus belonging in the early historical traditions about the ministry of Jesus.

Finally, there are the sacraments. That the primitive Church practised baptism 'into Christ' is difficult to doubt; that they broke bread as a memorial of Christ, is I think, indicated for even very early days. Are such rites explicable if Jesus was regarded simply as an individual—an honoured memory of the past? Does it not positively require the Pauline ἐν Χριστῷ to make explicit what is already implicit in the sacraments? Dr Beasley-Murray, it is true, argues[24] for baptism 'into Christ' (εἰς Χριστόν) meaning no more than into the name of Christ' (εἰς τὸ ὄνομα Χριστοῦ—like Hebrew, *l^eshem*), i.e. into his following. But it seems to me that the burden of proof rests on those who assume that the straight 'into' (εἰς) is identical with 'into the name' (εἰς τὸ ὄνομα); and I find Dr C. K. Barrett[25] more convincing when he suggests that the unusual baptism 'into

---

[24] *Baptism in the New Testament*, 1962, 128 f.
[25] *From First Adam to Last*, 1962, 49 f.

Moses' (εἰς τὸν Μωϋσῆν) of I Cor. 10.2 is not the Jewish model from which the Christian phrase came, but, on the contrary, is an abnormal phrase modelled on the striking Christian formula. One cannot, I think, argue from the converse—that 'into the name' (εἰς τὸ ὄνομα) is actually used with reference to Christ, meaning 'into his allegiance'—so as to establish that this is all that is meant by 'into Christ' (εἰς Χριστόν). 'Name'-phrases are, indeed, used in Acts (e.g. 2.38, ἐπί with dative; 8.16, εἰς); and in I Cor. 1, 13, 15 (the passage already cited) Paul, repudiating the notion of baptism into his own name, implies baptism into the name of Christ. But the use of a phrase of mere ownership or allegiance with reference to Christ does not negate the deeper meaning when a different phrase is used.

III. *Assessment*

If there is any cogency in this argument for a generally accepted Christian estimate of Jesus as an inclusive, incorporative personality, then we have a most remarkable phenomenon, which the unbeliever may justly be challenged to account for.

We must not overstate our case, as though the ἐν-formula (in relation not merely to God, which is common, and not surprising, but to a person of history or of legend) had not even verbal parallels elsewhere. As Dodd[26] reminds us, it is possible to find in classical Greek phrases describing one person (or even a group of persons) as 'in' another individual: in Sophocles, *Oedipus Tyrannus* 314, Oedipus appeals to Teiresias to save Thebes, and says ἐν σοὶ γάρ ἐσμεν ('for we are in you'). But this is only a verbal parallel, for it means 'we are in your hands', not 'we are incorporate in you'.

Again, it is true, and a familiar fact, probably for oriental thought generally and certainly for Hebrew thought, that it oscillates easily between the individual and the corporate, and that representative figures are viewed as gathering up into themselves the whole corporation—nation, tribe, or family—for which they stand. There is nothing new in that, and I have myself just been urging that Daniel's symbol of the human figure, the son of man, is essentially an inclusive one. There are, then, certain verbal parallels. But what remains extraordinary is not the concept of an individual figure summing up a corporate group, but the

[26] *The Interpretation of the Fourth Gospel*, 1953, 187 f.

identification of such an inclusive figure in a known, historical individual. The idea of being *in Adam* is, of course, well authenticated for non-Christian thought[27]; but that is tantamount to being in mankind, and is far different from alluding in such terms to a figure of recent history. Again, there are instances of patriarchal figures like Abraham or David, or figures of the then slightly less remote past like Hezekiah, being taken by Jewish thinkers as symbols of the people for whom they stood.[28] But I doubt whether even in reference to them a phrase like 'in David' or 'in Hezekiah' is instanced; and with heroes much nearer to the period I have never heard a hint of it: who ever heard of being 'in Judas Maccabaeus'? And as for Greek thought, not even the most ardent disciples, so far as I know, ever dreamt of being 'in Socrates'. Even with so symbolic a figure as the Emperor, I know of no instance of such a usage.

Perhaps, just possibly, this kind of language might have obtained in the early mystery cults: one can, I think, conceive of a Maenad being 'in Dionysus'. But, to the best of my knowledge, the evidence is precisely in the reverse direction—the direction which, as we have seen, is, in Christian terminology, much the rarer: the god is said to be in them, not they in the god; for that, it seems, is what ἔνθεος means—it means 'having the god within'. That, so far as I know, is the Hellenic notion of divine 'possession'.[29] How soon after Christianity we begin to find the full-blown language of mystical interpretation, is another question; but I do not know of any pre-Christian example.

How came it, then, just in this bunch of Jews—men and women

[27] Full details in J. Jervell, *Imago Dei*, 1960, 105 ff. Using Ps. 139.16 (*golmî*) certain Midrashes held that Adam was a great shapeless lump, from which God shaped all mankind; all mankind were *in him*.

[28] See E. Schweizer, 'Die Kirche als Leib Christi in den paulinischen Homologoumena', *ThLz*, 86.3, March 1961, 161 ff.; and 'Die Kirche . . . Antilegomena', *ThLz*, 86.4, April 1961, 241 ff.

[29] 'It is not quite clear whether the form ἔνθεος is the grammatical equivalent of ἐν θεῷ on the analogy of most adjectives of this formation, e.g. ἐντόπιος, ἔνδημιος, ἐνάλιος, ἐνόριος, ἔγκαιρος, etc., or whether it means "containing God", on the analogy of ἔμψυχος, ἔμπνους, ἐναίματος, ἔνοινος, ἔνσπορος, ἔγκαρπος [a footnote compares the English idiom "*in* his right mind", "*in* flower", etc.], and a few others. But as we have seen it matters little from which end the relation is regarded. In any case the meaning of ἔνθεος is well established. The adjective denotes possession by a god . . .' (C. H. Dodd. *The Interpretation of the Fourth Gospel*, 190; he illustrates this from Philo).

diverse in temperament and education, but alike in that they were all devout monotheists, having no inclinations towards paganism or mystery-cults—that this daring, this highly paradoxical conception sprang up? They began to regard the Rabbi, whom some of them had known personally, whom all of them knew of as a recently executed victim of injustice, as the body in which they were limbs. Can you conceive of Paul speaking of himself as 'in Gamaliel'? Whence, then, sprang this most unlikely sense?[30]

C. H. Dodd, at the end of a chapter on 'Son of Man',[31] wrote the following suggestive words: Christ's '"glory" is the transfiguration of a human life by a supreme act of self-sacrifice; He lays down His life for His friends, as many a man has done (xv. 13). And yet, says the evangelist, in all this He was much more than one individual among the many. He was the true self of the human race, standing in that perfect union with God to which others can attain only as they are incorporate in Him; the mind, whose thought is truth absolute (xiv. 6), which other men think after Him; the true life of man, which other men live by sharing it with Him (xiv. 6, vi. 57).

'It is clear that this conception raises a new problem. It challenges the mind to discover a doctrine of personality, which will make conceivable this combination of the universal and the particular in a single person. A naïve individualism regarding man, or a naïve anthropomorphism regarding God, makes nonsense of the Johannine Christology. Ancient thought, when it left the ground of such naïve conceptions, lost hold upon the concrete actuality of the person. It denied personality in man by making the human individual no more than an unreal "imitation" of the abstract universal Man, and it denied personality in God by making Him no more than the abstract unity of being. A Christian philosophy starting from the Johannine doctrine of Jesus (as Son of Man) should be able to escape the *impasse* into which all ancient thought fell, and to give an account of personality in God and in ourselves.'

I know that that relates specifically to the thought of the Fourth

[30] N. Turner, writing purely as a grammarian, says: 'We perceive then that it is from theology and Biblical syntax, and not from comparative syntax, that light is shed on this peculiar relationship expressed by ἐν; to compare non-Biblical parallels is largely irrelevant' (J. H. Moulton, *A Grammar of NT Greek*, iii, 1963, 263).

[31] *The Interpretation of the Fourth Gospel*, 249.

Gospel, where I would, for my part, be more reserved about the explicitness of the corporate idea. But the viewpoint which it summarizes is at least implicit (as I have tried to show) here and elsewhere in the New Testament, and, indeed, in the Christian estimate of Christ wherever it is found.

I must not now embark on the discussion of a new and immense question; but it is relevant at this point at least to set on record my belief that it is only this supra-individual estimate of Jesus that gives coherence to the New Testament presentation of the miracles—and, most of all, of the supreme miracle of the resurrection. I doubt whether one can ever hope to define, in modern terms, precisely what happened on any given occasion when Jesus is described as performing a 'mighty deed', a 'significant act'—a δύναμις or a σημεῖον; but I am sure that one cannot, without making nonsense of the whole Gospel story, eliminate from the traditions the sense that where Jesus was, there a titanic battle was always engaged in with the forces of evil. Both his words and his deeds are blows aimed at the very Kingdom of evil by the Kingdom of God himself. This means that Jesus represents a supra-individual conflict. And in the same way the resurrection is not the resuscitation of a mere individual, but victory over death won by New Man.

And so we are left asking: How came it that these Christians reached this astonishing 'combination of the universal and the particular in a single person' of recent history? If ancient thought offers no other instance of this, does not its emergence here point to a phenomenon of the foremost importance, and challenge the historian to tell us whence it originated?

III

THE JESUS OF TRADITION AND THE APOSTOLIC CHURCH: THE ARGUMENT FROM THE CONTINUITY BETWEEN 'THE JESUS OF HISTORY' AND 'THE LORD OF FAITH': I

Two phenomena have so far been displayed. First, the coming into existence of 'the sect of the Nazarenes'. I have tried to show that the very birth and survival of the Christian Church of the earliest days is significant evidence for the Christian claim. It is not evidence for some popular appeal or sustaining element of truth in the ideology or ethics of its members, for, as far as I can see, they had nothing here that was not common to Judaism. The only thing that launched and maintained them as distinctive was their witness to the risen Lord. That was the question by which they stood or fell. This fact presents a problem to those who are determined to regard that by which they stood or fell as a weak illusion.

I have urged, secondly, that a remarkable phenomenon is presented by the inability, evinced by the New Testament writers generally, to treat Jesus as merely an individual of the past—a revered example of days gone by. Without any surrender whatever of their conviction that he actually lived as *a* man, a vividly individual person, under a dateable Roman Governor, Pontius Pilate (indeed, in the very course of defending this conviction against attack by 'docetists', who wanted to treat Jesus as only a semblance of a man), they seem to have found themselves thinking of him, in one way or another, as also an inclusive, incorporative personality—just as they thought of God himself. Even making allowance for the familiar fact that Hebrew thought seems more easily to have oscillated between the individual and the collective than western thinking does, it remains a very extraordinary thing that devout, monotheistic Jews should have come to treat as divinely inclusive of themselves, as the Body of

43

which they were limbs and organs, an individual who had never held any representative office in Israel, and who, in their lifetime, had suffered a degrading execution. Such a phenomenon, I suggested, fairly shouts for attention, and poses extremely difficult questions to any serious historian who insists on trying to explain away the Christian faith.

And now, as a factor in a cumulative argument—for I would not claim that it would carry very much weight by itself—there is this little Aramaic word *Abba* and its implications.

This chapter and the next may, as I have suggested, be entitled, 'The Jesus of tradition and the Apostolic Church: the argument from the continuity between the Jesus of history and the Lord of faith'; and, were this our immediate task, it would be possible and necessary greatly to develop this particular theme. One of the most striking features, it seems to me, of the present phase in Gospel research is a trend in certain quarters towards the recovery of this continuity. If one were to put it schematically (and therefore, no doubt, without proper regard to the niceties of the facts) one might distinguish between the Jesus of history and the Lord of faith as two concepts; let us represent them by two circles on opposite sides of a dividing line:

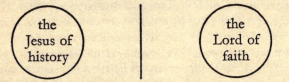

and one might say, in a rough-and-ready way, that the era of Liberal Protestant research—all the *Leben Jesu Forschung*, the research into the life of Jesus, reviewed by Albert Schweitzer in *The Quest of the Historical Jesus*—represented both the conviction that there was a great gulf fixed between the Jesus of history and the Lord of faith, and a vigorous preference for the former. 'Freedom from Paul' was the slogan of this movement: *los von Paulus*—let us get free from Paul and the 'catholicizing' theologians and get back to the simple Jesus of Galilee![1] This tendency could be graphically represented, then, by filling in the left-hand circle heavily as important and solid, as contrasted with the right-hand one, and making the dividing-line heavy and thick:

[1] See F. Prat, S.J., *The Theology of St Paul*, ET, 1945, ii, 22.

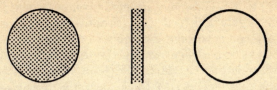

The opposite extreme—the great swing of the pendulum, represented, if you like, by Rudolf Bultmann—maintains the great gulf, but devotes all its attention to the hither side of it, to the Lord of faith as proclaimed in the apostolic kerygma: we know next to nothing, it says, of the Jesus of history; all the weight of our emphasis must fall on the preached Word. This means transferring the emphasis from the left circle to the right, and maintaining and increasing the thickness of the party-wall between them:

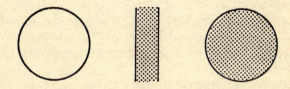

But there is discernible a post-Bultmannian trend. This has been discussed and characterized and criticized in numberless books and articles,[2] and it is all too easy to imagine that it is a palpable trend that can be defined and seized hold of. Actually, however, it is far too elusive and consists of far too many diverse factors to be pinned down with any certainty. And, in any case, before this ink is dry, there will, no doubt, be plenty of new factors emerging. But what I should, with all necessary reservations, say is discernible is the beginning of a recognition that the apostolic kerygma may and should be *tested* for its authenticity. That is, that the 'barrier' in our diagram can be, to some extent, seen through; that we have a right to ask: Are these apostolic confessions justified? What lies behind them? What can a historian reconstruct by deductions from them? And the answers to these questions seem, in certain quarters, to be

[2] J. M. Robinson's *A New Quest of the Historical Jesus*, 1959, is an important example of such discussion; but see also, for criticism of this movement, Carl E. Braaten's introductory essay in *Kerygma and History*, 1962, edited by Carl E. Braaten and Roy A. Harrisville.

beginning to be: Yes, the apostolic confessions are justified, because the figure which emerges from the most radically critical attempt at reconstruction is the figure of one whose teaching and message were of the very same quality as attaches to the figure of the apostolic proclamation. The Jesus retrieved by the most careful criticism (and it is, I think, perverse to assert that such critical reconstruction can accomplish nothing) is no longer the rationally acceptable moralist of the Liberal Protestants, but a 'catalyst'—a person whose very presence precipitates a crisis of faith and forces 'existential' decision. In an extremely interesting lecture,[3] W. Marxsen argues that what he calls the 'Christus-kerygma', the confessional proclamation about Jesus as Christ, ought to be tested by the 'Jesuskerygma'—the proclamation which critical scholarship is able to attribute to Jesus himself during his ministry. Otherwise, we have absolutely nothing to connect us with Jesus. And if the apostolic proclamation of Jesus as Christ is so tested, he says, we find that the 'Christus-kerygma' is saying, about the *death* of Jesus, what the 'Jesus-kerygma' says about the whole ministry, namely, that it brings men into the presence of God. Only, this process of testing has, of course, to work backwards from Easter, not forwards from the ministry. In a similar vein, O. Cullmann[4] points out that what the apostles remembered of Jesus' ministry included his own interpretation of it, however much and however often this had, at the time, been misunderstood. In a sense, the post-Easter *interpretation* was only a *re-discovery* of what had been there in the teaching of Jesus himself.

It would be easy enough to say that the reason why the Jesus now beginning to be recognized in this type of research is so different from the rational moralist of the Liberal Protestants is merely that the modern scholar is looking at things through his own presuppositions every bit as much as his predecessor was through his, and (to use the celebrated metaphor) that he is naturally seeing only his own reflection at the bottom of his deep well. It would be easy to say, in this vein, that the reason why today's reflection is so different is that today's scholar is a man with a different philosophy and theology. That the image is dif-

---

[3] 'Erwägungen zum Problem des verkundigten Kreuzes', *NTS*, 8.3, April 1962, 204 ff.

[4] *Heil als Geschichte*, 1965, 86.

ferent from what was seen fifty years ago is only due to a change in the viewer. But I do not think the matter is as subjective as that. The story of the critical study of the parables, from Adolf Jülicher to Joachim Jeremias and beyond,[5] is enough to show that the change is due partly to actually improved knowledge of the contemporary background of the life of Christ and partly to improved techniques of research—in particular, to the application of form-criticism.

Thus, qualify the statement as one may (and, indeed, must), it is true that some not inconsiderable groups of scholars are daring once more, in a sense, to look back to the Jesus of history; but now they are finding, not the Liberal Protestant figure but a figure as challenging, as supernatural, as divine, as is found on the hither side in the apostolic Gospel: which means that the barrier between the two sides in our diagram is thinning, and the continuity increasing. The two circles have come to resemble one another more closely, and the dividing line is much less heavy. Dare one speculate that, one of these days, they might come even to coincide?[6]

But I have no intention of pursuing this theme any further in general: only of illustrating something of this continuity in one or two particular respects; and first, in respect of a subtle coherence, focussed in the word *Abba*, between Jesus' own conception of his relation to God and men during his ministry (so far as it may be recovered by critical discernment), and what St Paul and others believed about the relation of men to God through Christ.[7]

The word *Abba* occurs only three times in the New Testament, at Mark 14.36, Romans 8.15, and Galatians 4.6. The remarkable facts about it, for our purposes, are that it is addressed to God; and that, in the Pauline occurrences, it—an Aramaic word—is

---

[5] Well told in G. V. Jones' *The Art and Truth of the Parables*, 1964.

[6] *Contra* Carl E. Braaten in *Kerygma and History*, 21: 'Can the historian *qua* historian establish the continuity of the kerygma with antecedent history on purely historical grounds? . . . Kähler thought it nothing less than naïve and preposterous for the historian to establish the ground and the content of faith. Is this not precisely what the modern historians are attempting, however, when they set out to establish a continuity or identity between the earthly Jesus and the post-Easter Christ of the kerygma?'

[7] This theme has most recently been treated very fully in J. Jeremias' collected essays entitled *Abba: Studien zur neutestamentlichen Theologie und Zeitgeschichte*, 1966 (ET, *The Prayers of Jesus*, 1967).

apparently quite gratuitously embedded in the alien texture of a Greek letter. On the lips of Jesus and in a narrative, even when the narrative is in Greek, it is more understandable: there are one or two other fragments of his very language embedded in the traditions, for instance, *talitha cumi* and *ephphatha*. But that it should be gratuitously retained, untranslated, in a Greek letter is striking.

That it is addressed to God is remarkable, not because it means 'Father' (for already this conception of God is familiar in the Old Testament and Judaism) but because of its particular form. In a good many places the Old Testament likens God to a Father; once or twice it takes the further step of actually calling him a Father—moving, so to speak, from simile to metaphor. The Jewish liturgy today, preserving a form which seems to be agreed to go back as far, probably, as the first century AD, addresses God as 'Our Father, our King'.[8]

The idea of God as Father, and even the liturgical address to him as Father, is thus not distinctive of Christianity. But so far no instance has been found, we are told, of the use in prayer, public or private, of this particular form, *Abba*. This word has frequently been described[9] as, morphologically speaking, a *definite* form (literally meaning 'the father'), which had come to do duty for 'my father', during the obsolescence of the form (*abi*—see Dan. 5.13) which properly meant 'my father'. But Jeremias[10] shows that this is an inaccurate account. The *ā* in *abbā* does not represent the attached article of the definite form, the *status emphaticus*, which, incidentally, ought to be represented in transliteration by *abbā*; rather, this *abbā* is formed simply on the analogy of the corresponding *immā* for 'Mother'.[11] It is a child's word; and it seems to have been used in ordinary family life, but never (so far as our information goes) in direct address to God, except on the lips, first of Jesus, and then of Christians; and even Christians soon reverted to the standardized Jewish form 'our Father in

---

[8] *âbînû malkēnû* does not belong to the *earliest* form of the Eighteen Benedictions, but even so need not be *late* (cf. the Hebrew of Ecclus. 51.12—though that is itself an addition to the original). See K. G. Kuhn, *Achtzehngebet und Vaterunser und der Reim*, Tübingen 1950, 9, 13.

[9] See e.g., G. Dalman, *Grammatik des jüd.-palästin. Aramäisch*, ²1905, 90 f.; *The Words of Jesus*, ET, 1909, 192; S-B., ii, 49; G. Kittel in *TDNT* i, 5.

[10] *Abba*, 59 f.; *The Prayers of Jesus*, 58.

[11] Though Dalman in *Grammatik*, claims that this, too, is the definite form.

heaven', represented by the Matthean version of the Lord's prayer (Matt. 6.9 ff.),[12] in contrast to the Lucan version (Luke 11.2 ff., which, according to what is perhaps the best reading, has simply 'Father'), which probably represents more faithfully the simple, family address of the original.

Admittedly, this is an argument from silence to the extent that actual prayer-forms need not necessarily be frequent even in so extensive a range of Jewish literature as is at our disposal. However, as far as it goes, the evidence is clear enough: 'I have examined the whole later Jewish literature of prayer', wrote Jeremias (in an earlier treatment),[13] 'and the result was that in no place in this immense literature is this invocation of God to be found. The Church Fathers Chrysostom, Theodor[e], and Theodoret, who originated from Antioch and had Aramaic-speaking nurses, tell us that *abba* was the address of a small child to his father.'[14]

It looks, then, as though it was Jesus himself who first dared to use this very simple, family address in his prayer to God. It is one of the three or four Aramaic words and phrases preserved in the traditions of the words of Jesus. But it is still more striking when St Paul uses the same Aramaic word (as he does in Rom. 8, Gal. 4) to describe what it is that the Holy Spirit enables Greek-speaking Christians to say.[15]

Let me say at once, returning for a moment to the Lord's

[12] Cf. the late Targumic instances of '*abba* in heaven', cited by G. Kittel, *TDNT*, i, 5.

[13] 'The Lord's Prayer in Modern Research', *ExpT* lxxi, 5, Feb. 1960, 141 ff. (see 144).

[14] For this, see T. Zahn, *Forschungen zur Geschichte des neutestamentlichen Kanons*, i, 1881, 41, where he says that only one who had grown up in a town where nurses would be Syrians could, like Theodoret on Rom. 8.15, have observed that the little children often addressed their fathers so. (See Migne, *Patrologia Graeca*, 82, Col. 133: τὰ γάρ τοι παιδία πλείονι παρρησίᾳ κεχρημένα πρὸς τοὺς πατέρας (οὐδέπω γὰρ τελείαν τὴν διάκρισιν ἔχει), συχνότερον πρὸς αὐτοὺς τῇδε κέχρηται τῇ φωνῇ.) In his commentary on Romans, 1910, 395, n. 93, he guesses that all three Church Fathers mentioned would have had Syrian nurses. The references for the other two are given by Jeremias, *Abba* (as on p. 47, n. 7), 61, n. 41; *The Prayers of Jesus*, 60, n. 41; Chrysostom, *Hom. in Ep. ad Rom.* 14 (on Rom. 8.15), Migne, *PG* 60, Col. 527: ὅπερ τῶν παίδων μάλιστά ἐστιν τῶν γνησίων πρὸς πατέρα ῥῆμα (but this is not explicit about its being a baby-word); Theodore of Mopsuestia, *Comm. on Rom.* 8.15, Migne, *PG* 66, Col. 824: τῶν νηπίων ἴδιόν ἐστι τὸ ἀββᾶ καλεῖν τοὺς πατέρας.

[15] The addition of the Greek, ὁ πατήρ, is curious. J. V. McCasland, *JBL*, lxxii, 1953, 79 ff., claims that the two are not synonymous. J. Lagrange,

prayer, that I am inclined to believe that the Lord's prayer, as Jesus originally taught it to his disciples, began in just this way. I have already said that I believe that the Lucan version of the Lord's prayer, in its best text, begins not 'Our Father . . .' (like the Jewish liturgical form), but πάτερ simply, which would well represent *Abba*. If this is true, then away go the sermons which make a point out of the introduction, 'After this manner therefore pray ye . . .' (as though Jesus did not mean to include himself), and then go on to make a further point out of the first person plural in the invocation, 'Our Father . . .'.[16] No: I believe that there is no stress to be laid on the 'ye', and that originally (although the verbs and the pronouns of the prayer are undeniably in the first person plural) there was no '*our* Father *in heaven*' in the opening invocation, but simply this brief, deeply intimate, children's word *Abba*.[17] It may even be that when St Paul alludes to the word he does so because the entire Lord's prayer was still current in its Aramaic form; but I am not sure whether that is the natural deduction. At any rate, my immediate point is that in this address to God, Jesus seems to have laid no particular emphasis on any distinction between himself and his disciples; he enjoined on them the same intimate address as he himself dared to use; and, according to Paul, this striking intimacy had been duly carried over into Christian prayer-habits.

Incidentally, I would wish to argue similarly for John 20.17, where Jesus' message to the disciples is: 'I am ascending to my Father and your Father, to my God and your God.' We need not stay over the question whether a genuine saying of Jesus is preserved here or not. All I wish to point out is that, whereas the phrase has sometimes been construed as deliberately calling attention to a distinction of status between Jesus and the dis-

---

S. Marc, 1929, 388, suggests, as just possible, that Jesus himself may have uttered both words, on the analogy of *mārī qīrī*, a Semitic phrase in which *qīrī* is a transliteration of the Greek, κύριε. But he admits that it is more natural to assume that *abba* was followed, in early Christian catechesis, by its Greek translation.

[16] E.g., E. Lohmeyer, *The Lord's Prayer*, ET, 1965, of *Das Vater-Unser*, 1952, 52.

[17] See e.g., G. Bornkamm, *Jesus of Nazareth*, ET, 1960, of *Jesus von Nazareth*, ³1959, 128 f. K. G. Kuhn in *Achtzehngebet und Vaterunser und der Reim*, 32, renders the Lucan form into Aramaic, starting with simply *abba!* What I have said is intended to apply to the address to God. I do not mean to suggest that Jesus himself would have felt the need to ask for forgiveness.

ciples, comparable to the falsely-supposed distinction between Christ's own 'My Father' and the disciples' 'Our Father' in the Lord's prayer, it can equally well, or more plausibly, be construed in precisely the opposite sense, to stress the identity of approach between Christ and the disciples: 'my Father *who is also* your Father, my God *who is also* yours'. I do not think that this type of Greek requires the definite article which strictly correct classical usage might for such a sense.[18]

So much, then, for the daring identity of intimacy preserved by the Christian Church in their repetition of the term *Abba*—perhaps actually in the Lord's prayer—and reflected, it may be, in other sayings.[19]

But there is also a difference. And my main point is precisely that both the difference and the identity are reflected—with no deliberate collaboration or premeditation on the matter between the writers of different parts of the New Testament. Both the difference and the identity are reflected on both sides, both in the Gospels when they portray the ministry of Jesus and in the post-resurrection Church. Some would, of course, say that this is nothing but a recognition that the Gospels are themselves theological and unhistorical and therefore naturally chime in with the theological outlook of the epistles. But the facts are not so simple. It is quite impossible to eliminate the striking difference in perspective between the Synoptic Gospels and the rest of the New Testament, or to bring all their traditions into the mould of *Gemeindetheologie*, the theology of the Christian community after the death of Christ. To explain the coincidence so would be to ignore all the differences.

Accordingly, any coincidence of viewpoint between the two, in respect of the status of Jesus and of his followers, is significant; and it is striking, therefore, that, while St Paul preserves the *Abba*, he attributes it to a Spirit of *adoption* (Rom. 8.15) or the Spirit of God's Son (Gal. 4.6): he recognizes it as derived rather than inherent.

I take it that by 'a Spirit of adoption' ($\pi\nu\epsilon\hat{\upsilon}\mu\alpha$ $\upsilon\iota\upsilon\theta\epsilon\sigma\iota\alpha\varsigma$) St Paul meant (using one of those allusive and highly-charged genitives for which he is notorious) that the Spirit of God is a

---

[18] For the sense, cf. Rom. 16.13: $\tau\grave{\eta}\nu$ $\mu\eta\tau\acute{\epsilon}\rho\alpha$ $\alpha\grave{\upsilon}\tauο\hat{\upsilon}$ $\kappa\alpha\grave{\iota}$ $\grave{\epsilon}\mu o\hat{\upsilon}$—'his mother, who is also a mother to me'.

[19] Cf., strikingly, John 12.28: $\pi\alpha\tau\acute{\epsilon}\rho$, $\delta\acute{o}\xi\alpha\sigma\acute{o}\nu$ $\sigma o\upsilon$ $\tau\grave{o}$ $\acute{o}\nu o\mu\alpha$—'Father, glorify your name!'—strongly reminiscent of the Lord's prayer.

Spirit leading us to adoption as sons—a Spirit which compasses our adoption into the family. It is (to turn to the Galatians form of the remark) the Spirit of God's Son which utters, in us, Christ's own '*Abba!*' In other words, the ability to cry this cry of deepest intimacy and of absolute obedience arises from the presence of the Spirit of God in us as the Spirit of his own Son. It is therefore a derived sonship—an adoption.[20]

It is true, I know, that there seems to have been no such word as υἱότης, 'sonship', by this period: the term 'sonship', so dear to Christology today, was (apparently) not available: and it could be argued, therefore, that St Paul used 'adoption', loosely, to mean 'sonship'. Does not St Paul himself, later on in Rom. 8 (v. 29), dare to call Christ our elder brother—πρωτότοκος ἐν πολλοῖς ἀδελφοῖς—'the eldest of a large family'? But I believe that the distinction between the '*birthright*' of the eldest and the only derivative status of the rest is clear; and that the burden of proof rests on those who want to equate 'adoption', υἱοθεσία (a word evidently chosen by Paul from the pagan world, for it has no exact equivalent in the Old Testament), with the un-attested 'sonship', υἱότης. It is a striking fact that the Johannine writings, in their different idiom, preserve the same distinction by reserving one word for 'son', namely υἱός, for Jesus, and using another, namely, τέκνον or τεκνίον, for disciples.

What we have found then in Paul and John is, for believers, a deep but derived and secondary sonship, by baptism into the Name of Christ and by the sending of the Spirit; but for Jesus himself both Gospels and epistles reflect an *absolute* sonship. He is the fountain head, the ἀρχή (Col. 1.18), of this relationship, associated indeed, in the Synoptic stories of Jesus' baptism, with the Spirit, but in a unique and signal visitation.

We have noted in the Gospels the evidence that Jesus embraced his disciples in his instructions to approach God in terms of simplest intimacy as *Abba*. But now, returning again to the territory of the Gospels, we discover that, side by side with this, go traditions of that unique and lonely absoluteness and primacy

---

[20] '. . . Paul, in speaking of the "Sons of God", never makes mention of this except by speaking at the same time of the sending of "the Son". . . . Not in the strength of their own nature, but by the power of the "Spirit" who cries in their hearts the believers' cry: "Abba! Father!". . . .'—G. Born-kamm, *Jesus of Nazareth*, 129.

of the relation between Jesus as *the* Son, *par excellence*, and the Father. There is the divine voice at the baptism and at the transfiguration—extremely difficult, to my mind, to dismiss as something simply imposed on the traditions by the later theologizing of the Church. There is the profound significance of the narrative of the Temptations, all turning on the true and the false conceptions of Sonship. There are the hints scattered over the Marcan tradition—the address of Jesus by demons as Son of God; the hint at the climax of the parable of the wicked husbandmen (which, as Jeremias allows,[21] must, to Jesus himself, though not to his hearers, have signified his own sending); the use of the absolute terms, 'the Son', 'the Father' in Mark 13.32; and the declaration before the Sanhedrin (Mark 14.62); of the heavenly session—a saying in which the royal Figure of Ps. 110, seated at the right hand of God, is fused, perhaps, with the Son of Ps. 2 and with the vindicated martyr-figure of Daniel 7.[22] Finally, there is the famous 'Q' passage, Matthew 11.25–30, Luke 10.21–24, with its declaration of the mutual knowledge of Father and Son. This is a hotly disputed passage, and scholarship is still divided over the question of its originality; and of course the radical sayings in St John's Gospel fall under acute suspicion also. But the cumulative weight of these hints from many different levels and antiquities in the tradition is, I think, impressive. It looks as though here was one who perhaps seldom or never expressly *claimed* a title for himself except that of the suffering and eclipsed martyr Son of Man; but who *behaved* with the mastery appropriate to one who was heir to the whole Kingdom, and who occasionally lifted the veil of his self-consciousness to reveal just this at the heart of his vocation.

Thus we have in the Gospel traditions evidence of precisely the same subtle duality as is reflected, though in a different and independent way, in the epistles: a unique and natural status of Sonship belonging to Jesus, into which he gathers his disciples by adoption, so that they too dared, until ecclesiastical and liturgical timidity overtook them and stifled it, to use the very word *Abba* which Jesus had himself (if the argument is sound) first adopted for prayer to God.

[21] *The Parables of Jesus*, ET revised edition, 1963, 72 f.
[22] See E. Lövestam, *Son and Saviour*, 1961, 88 ff., for an important discussion of this.

Now, I realize that it would only be a very keen and attentive inquirer who would be willing to follow the details of this argument: but if his attention could be held, it adds, I believe, impressive support to the Christian position. It means that there is an apparently undesigned and totally unpremeditated coincidence between the Gospel tradition and the Pauline and Johannine outlooks in respect of a very subtle triangular relationship as between Christ and God and Christians: a relationship, moreover, which is deeply and organically and satisfyingly coherent with the whole doctrine of the Holy Spirit and the status of Christ as it emerges from the New Testament documents.

This provides independent confirmation of precisely that inclusive personality which we saw evidenced by the 'in Christ', ἐν Χριστῷ, or its equivalents, in the New Testament documents.

Let me add one further example from St Paul of the attitude we have been tracing. In II Cor. 1.20 Paul says that in Christ is the 'yes', the affirmation, to all God's promises; and that, he adds, is why it is through Christ that we utter the *Amen* to God. We are evidently overhearing a formula of early Christian prayer: it ends 'through Christ Jesus thy Son (v. 19), Amen'. In John 16.24, 26 there is even more explicit reference to prayer to the Father in the name of Christ—prayer to a Father who himself loves and is eager to give (vv. 26 f.). All this points to precisely the same relationship—the trustful recognition of God as Father, the intimacy and boldness of approach implicit in '*Abba*', coupled with that sense that it is, for the Christian, *derived* through the *absolute* Son, Jesus Christ. Again then, this retention by the Christian Church of the '*Abba*', and the 'through Jesus Christ' formula side by side bears striking witness to exactly that estimate of Jesus which is implicit in the other phenomena we have examined. Could so unaffected and seemingly unpremeditated a *theological* agreement be explained without a substantial common origin? We shall return, later, to the *Amen* to note a subtle difference between the usage of Jesus and the usage of the Church. But that is not relevant at the moment.

The phenomena I have just described are of immense importance, incidentally, for the study of the doctrine of the Trinity. This is a subject for which I have too little competence, even if there were time and space for it in the present study. But I have long believed that the '*Abba*' of St Mark's Gospel and of

St Paul's epistles is at the very heart of the New Testament doctrine of the Holy Spirit; and that the relation of Jesus to God and to the Spirit, compared and contrasted with the relation of believers to God in Christ by the power of the Holy Spirit, is the right starting-point for a study of the origins of the doctrine of the Trinity.

But I must leave this simply as a hint thrown out in passing.

IV

THE JESUS OF TRADITION AND THE APOSTOLIC CHURCH: THE ARGUMENT FROM THE CONTINUITY BETWEEN 'THE JESUS OF HISTORY' AND 'THE LORD OF FAITH': II

THUS far, three phenomena have been offered for consideration: the emergence of the Christian Church, the emergence of a corporate understanding of Christ, and the fact that an intimate relationship between Jesus and God, compared and contrasted with a similar but derived relationship among Christians, emerges both in the Gospels and in Paul. This third phenomenon constitutes one of several phenomena which seem to point to a genuine continuity between, on the one hand, the most primitive traditions about Jesus and, on the other hand, theological reflection about him. With such phenomena I now continue.

Luke contrasted with Acts

Recently, the differences between the presentation of Jesus in Luke's Gospel and in the Acts respectively were brought home to me in a special way. Having accepted an invitation to write a paper on the Christology of the Acts, I found myself conducting the inquiry by way of a series of comparisons. I compared the Acts, in respect of its Christology, with the Pauline writings, with I Peter, with Hebrews, and with the Johannine writings. I have already had occasion to mention one of the features which stands out sharply in Luke's Christology as compared with that of Paul—its individualism.[1] But what was, to me, the most interesting part of the investigation was the comparison of Luke with Luke. On the assumption that Acts is by the same hand as the Gospel, it was of obvious importance to compare the Christology of Acts with that of the same writer's Gospel—of obvious im-

[1] See pp. 36 ff., above, where I argue that, in spite of this, the conception of Christ as an inclusive person shows through.

portance as an objective test of what we are so used to hearing, namely, that even the Synoptic Gospels, let alone St John's Gospel, are written out of a fully developed faith and with all the post-resurrection assumptions.

Now, it is true, of course, that the Gospels were written after the death of Jesus and from within the early Church. But, more than that, we are told that they were written to interpret the Easter faith, and that they have, therefore, introduced anachronously into their story of the ministry of Jesus an estimate of him which did not emerge until later. Well, here, in a comparison of Luke's Gospel with Luke's Acts, we have an objective test of whether or not this Evangelist, at any rate, has thrown the whole of his Easter faith back anachronously into his narrative of what happened before Easter.

The answer is, that Luke does not attribute to the participants in his story of the ministry of Jesus the same explicit estimate of Jesus as he attributes to the apostles when they are speaking of the risen Jesus. That is to say, he represents the contemporaries of Jesus in his earthly life as speaking of him with reserve. They do not use the great Christological titles of the post-resurrection preaching. Yet, equally, Luke leaves not a shadow of doubt that the one to whom the exalted titles of the Church's proclamation are applied is the same man, Jesus of Nazareth, about whom he tells his story in his Gospel.

At the outset, one fact about Luke's handling of this theme is worth recording, if only because it happens to be frequently misrepresented. We are often told that Luke is the one, of all the Evangelists, who applies the title 'Lord' (κύριος) to Jesus during his ministry and before his death and exaltation. This is scarcely true. The use of the vocative, κύριε, as a respectful address, is not relevant to this question. In the vocative, it seems to be the commonest of polite addresses, and need, in itself, mean no more than 'Sir'; and, in any case, the other Evangelists also use the vocative, and Luke is not peculiar here. It would not be right to deduce from an English school-story in which the boys addressed the Headmaster as 'Sir' that he had been knighted. But the application of the word κύριος in its other cases, which might, indeed, be significant, is almost entirely absent, in Luke's Gospel, from the language of the *dramatis personae*. That the Evangelist himself refers to Jesus as 'the Lord' is true, but is not relevant to his reconstruction of the scene of the ministry itself. When he himself uses κύριος in his narrative this is no more importing the title into the scene of the ministry than if a modern writer said, 'The Lord was never actually called "Lord" during his ministry.' Luke, writing as a Christian, is committing no historical solecism by choosing this title for his own editorial statements.[2] But on the lips of actual participants in the action, it is the rarest exception. Luke—and, for that matter, Matthew and Mark also—represent Jesus as quoting Ps. 110 in such a way that 'my Lord' is made to refer to him. But that is an oblique hint. Otherwise, in Luke's Gospel, there are only the following exceptions. Elizabeth says to Mary, 'How comes it that the Mother of *my Lord* should come to me?' (1.43); Zechariah speaks of John as going before 'the Lord' (1.76, which the Christian reader interprets as the Lord Jesus—but if there is a genuine original in John the Baptist's traditions, it no doubt meant God); and Jesus himself uses it of himself, in the instructions to his disciples about the colt, and they accordingly repeat it ('the Lord needs it', 19.31, 34). Otherwise, the title is used only by the angel in the shepherds' annunciation (2.11), until the resurrection, when, at once, 'the Lord' comes upon the lips of disciples: Luke 24.34.

Now this point must not be made too much of. I record it as a fact, because the fact is so often overlooked. But, admittedly, it so happens that there is virtually no room, in the structure of the Gospel, for references to Jesus, in the third person, by participants in the action who are well-disposed towards him, until the death. It is all dialogue, in the second person, between Jesus and his friends. His friends are almost never shown speaking about him to others. So, it could be argued that the very few exceptions just cited are highly significant. They are exceptions precisely because they constitute the only references to Jesus in the third person by participants in the action, and it is, therefore, more significant that ὁ κύριος does appear in these cases, though they are few, than that it is absent where there is no occasion for it to be used. This may be a fair point; but, even if it be allowed, it does not

---

[2] Interestingly enough, almost the same is true of St John's Gospel. In certain narrative references (4.1; 6.23; 11.2, suspected, as a matter of fact, of being interpolations by another hand) Jesus is referred to as ὁ κύριος. But the participants in the drama itself are not credited with using the title till the resurrection. It has to be admitted, however, that Mary Magdalene is credited with using the title before she *knows* that Jesus has risen (20.13).

alter the fact that it is a misstatement to represent Luke as habitually letting Jesus be called Lord in his pre-resurrection story; and, anyway, there are other phenomena which indicate fairly clearly that the author of Luke-Acts registers a change in the explicit estimate of Jesus by his friends as between the period of the ministry and its sequel.

This is not the place to go into the detail which appears in another publication.[3] But certain other phenomena may be mentioned briefly. There is a subtle but consistent difference in the use of the term 'prophet' as between the Gospel and the Acts. It is not until the Acts (3.22 f. and 7.37, by clear implication) that Jesus is identified as '*the* Prophet like Moses', of Deut. 18.15. In the Gospel, he is simply *a* prophet—and that, in the eyes of disbelievers or the disillusioned (Luke 7.16, 39; 9.8, 19; 24.19), or where Jesus alludes to himself as among the prophets (4.24; 13.33). The only exception is in the subtle implications of the divine voice at the transfiguration, where 'listen to him' (Luke 9.35) may be an allusion to Deut. 18.15. If so, then this divine recognition of Jesus as *the* Moses-prophet is analogous to the use of κύριος in the angelic announcement. The use of 'Elijah' is even more subtle, and to that I want to return later, in a wider context than that of Luke's version.

The confining of the use of an exalted title for Jesus, in the period of the ministry, to the more than human participants is again illustrated by the use of 'Saviour' and 'Son of God'. 'Saviour' occurs, in the Gospel, only on the lips of the angel (2.11), although Simeon certainly associates God's act of deliverance (σωτήριον) with the child Jesus (2.30), and the disillusioned two on the way to Emmaus refer to their dashed hopes: it was he, so they had hoped, who was going to ransom Israel (24.21). But in the Acts 'there is no other name under heaven granted to men, by which we may receive salvation' (σωτηρία), 4.12; and in 5.31 and 13.23 (Peter and Paul respectively) the title 'Saviour' is used explicitly. Again, 'Son of God' is used in St Luke's Gospel only by other than human voices—divine, angelic, or satanic (1.32, 35; 3.22; 4.3, 9, 41; 8.28); or by Jesus himself in his monologue (10.22), until the climax of the story, at the trial before the Sanhedrin (22.70)—although the reply of Jesus even there may

[3] 'The Christology of Acts', in *Studies in Luke-Acts* (in honour of Paul Schubert), ed. Leander E. Keck and J. Louis Martyn, 1966, 159 ff.

be intended to be non-committal. But in Acts, Paul is represented as explicitly affirming the title (9.20; 13.33; cf. 8.37 in the δ-text).

By contrast, there is the notorious fact that 'the Son of Man' is a term confined by all the Evangelists (even John 12.34 is no real exception) to the sayings of Jesus himself, except in the one instance of the dying Stephen in Acts 7.56. We all know how hotly it is debated whether Jesus himself used the term 'the Son of Man', and, if so, whether he even applied it to himself—and, in any case, what may have been the equivalent in Aramaic and what it may have meant. But nobody will doubt that the Evangelists themselves believed that Jesus used it, and used it of himself; and (apart from the use of a comparable phrase in Rev. 1.13; 14.14, where it is clearly drawn direct from Dan. 7, and the use of υἱὸς ἀνθρώπου from Ps. 8 in Heb. 2.6) Acts 7.56 is the only example in all the New Testament of its use as a title for Jesus by another. The martyr Stephen declares that he sees the heavens opened and the Son of Man standing at the right hand of God. Much has been written about this unusual use: the Son of Man *standing* (not *seated* as in Mark 14.62, where Ps. 110 seems to be fused with Dan. 7), and hailed as such by another.[4] My own guess still[5] is that it is the martyr-context which accounts for both peculiarities. Normally, the post-resurrection Church did not find 'the Son of Man' an appropriate title for the risen Lord. It was right for his sufferings and privations on earth (corresponding to the persecution of the 'saints' in Dan. 7.21). It was right for his future coming with the clouds (Rev. 1.13; 14.14); but in the meantime it is appropriate only where the suffering Church on earth gives its witness to Christ: and at such a point the Danielic figure may be seen in the heavenly court, standing, like a witness in a law-court, to vindicate his faithful witness on earth. The reservation of the term to this context and the subtle variation of phrase in Acts 7.56 seem to me to bear witness to the writer's clear consciousness of a changed situation as between the period of the ministry of Jesus and the period of the apostolic Church, as well

---

[4] See e.g., besides the standard Christologies and monographs on the Son of Man etc., H. P. Owen, 'Stephen's Vision in Acts vii. 55–56', *NTS*, 1.3, 1955, 224 ff. (Jesus is standing as though to return to earth); C. K. Barrett, 'Stephen and the Son of Man', in *Apophoreta* (Festschrift for E. Haenchen, ed. W. Eltester, 1964), 32 ff. (a private and personal *parousia* for the individual as he dies).   [5] See Appendix I, pp. 90 f.

as to a genuine continuity between the earthly and the risen Jesus.

One other feature furnishing both contrast and bond of connexion as between the Gospel and the Acts is the way in which the Holy Spirit is referred to. In the Gospel, Jesus is represented as himself uniquely endowed with Spirit (as in the story of his baptism), but not as bestowing the Spirit. The same is true of the miniature 'Gospel' to Cornelius in Acts 10, where Jesus is described as 'anointed' by God with Holy Spirit and power (v. 38). But in the Acts narrative itself, Jesus, as exalted Lord, pours out the Spirit (2.33); and, indeed, the preaching to Cornelius itself provides precisely the same contrast in miniature: in 10.36 Jesus is first introduced by the most exalted title, 'Lord of all', πάντων κύριος; then comes the 'Gospel-like' account of the ministry, which we have just looked at, in which we are back in the pre-resurrection categories (vv. 37–39); and then comes reference to the resurrection (vv. 40 f.), to the consequent commission to evangelize, and to the judgeship of Jesus and forgiveness in his name, by faith (vv. 42 f.); and then the Holy Spirit falls on Cornelius and his company. The sequence is consistently observed.

Now, of course, we all know that it is possible for an Evangelist to create a contrast of this sort artificially. Ever since William Wrede's celebrated book,[6] the world of New Testament scholarship has been familiar with the idea of an artificial messianic secret, devised, in the case of Mark—so Wrede suggested—as a way of expressing the fundamental hiddenness and challenge to faith implicit in Jesus. But it is a question whether even the 'messianic secret' in Mark really yields to this sort of treatment; and the cumulation of subtle differences-with-continuity which I have alluded to in the case of Luke, where we have a test case in a writer who occupies, as it were, both territories, seems to me very difficult indeed to explain as an artificial construction. It seems easier and more reasonable to look, rather, for some cataclysmic event, after and beyond which the same Jesus is recognized in a new way and in a transcendent capacity.

Features in tradition surviving against opposition

This may be styled, in a sense, a negative phenomenon—the

[6] *Das Messiasgeheimnis in den Evengelien. Zugleich ein Beitrag zum Verständnis des Markusevangeliums,* 1901.

absence of apparent anachronisms. We have seen an evangelist refusing to credit the *dramatis personae* of his narrative of the ministry with an estimate of Jesus which had only arisen subsequently. We have witnessed in him something (however incomplete it may be) of the reserve that a modern historian might exercise in trying to exclude anachronisms from his reconstruction. But perhaps even more impressive is what may be called a positive phenomenon. By this I mean the phenomenon of a feature in the tradition asserting itself despite a tendency in its transmitters militating against it. It is one thing to avoid importing into one's narrative value judgments reached at a period subsequent to what it describes. It is another thing to retain in that narrative features which conflict with current estimates. It would appear that there are certain features in the story of Jesus, the retention of which can scarcely be explained except by their genuineness and durable quality, since everything else was hostile to their survival.

This is the principle seized on by P. W. Schmiedel in his famous article, 'Gospels', in *Encyclopaedia Biblica*.[7] He (§139) regarded as solid foundation-pillars of a historical reconstruction such sayings of Jesus as were evidently alien to the outlook and tendencies of the Evangelists themselves, namely: Mark 3.21 (Jesus' relatives think him mad); 10.18 ('Why do you call me good?'); Matt. 12.31 f. (blasphemy against the Son of Man is forgivable); Mark 13.32 (Jesus' ignorance of the time of the End); 15.34 (the cry of dereliction). To these sayings of Jesus he adds (§140) certain sayings about Jesus also. Modern scholarship has accepted the principle,[8] although without concentrating on Schmiedel's particular instances. Attention tends now to be directed to the more radical sayings of Jesus which have, as it were, been let through here and there in the stream of tradition, while in other channels they have been modified or expunged.

The Marcan form of the Great Commandment

An arresting example, seized on by, among others, E. Stauffer,[9] is the Marcan form of Jesus' saying on the great commandment,

---

[7] *Encyclopaedia Biblica*, ed T. K. Cheyne and J. S. Black, 1899–1903.

[8] It is essentially the same principle as that formulated by M. Bloch, see above, p. 7.

[9] *Die Botschaft Jesu damals und heute*, 1959, 44 ff.

as compared with the versions in Matthew and Luke. In Mark 12.28 ff. it is absolutely uncompromising: Love of God and love of neighbour are the great commandments: than these, there is none greater (μείζων τούτων ἄλλη οὐκ ἔστιν)—which means that nothing whatever must stand in the way of their discharge. The startling radicalism of such a position over against the legalism of certain sections of devout Judaism is obvious enough, and would help to account for the violent opposition which Jesus seems to have encountered from the Pharisees. It may be significant that in Luke's version this exclusive clause is simply lacking. But Matthew, even more significantly, modifies it. Matthew 22.40 adds a sentence which makes it possible to understand the saying to mean that love of God and love of neighbour are not the exclusive but rather the basic or dominant principles, from which the rest of the legal system may be deduced: 'on these two commands the whole law and the prophets depend'. It is plausibly suggested that here we can detect the softening of an almost unendurably radical pronouncement. It is made to say that the legal system is not overridden by Jesus' answer but, on the contrary, may be deduced from it.

Jesus and the Women of the Gospels

In the above instance, Mark alone has retained the full stringency of the saying. But there is another aspect of the life and character of Jesus which seems to have asserted itself in all the traditions, despite an environment to which it seems likely to have been alien. This is Jesus' attitude to women and his relations with them. It is difficult enough for anyone, even a consummate master of imaginative writing, to create a picture of a deeply pure, good person moving about in an impure environment, without making him a prig or a prude or a sort of 'plaster saint'. How comes it that, through all the Gospel traditions without exception, there comes a remarkably firmly-drawn portrait of an attractive young man moving freely about among women of all sorts, including the decidedly disreputable, without a trace of sentimentality, unnaturalness, or prudery, and yet, at every point, maintaining a simple integrity of character? Is this because the environments in which the traditions were preserved and through which they were transmitted were peculiarly favourable to such a portrait?

On the contrary, it seems that they were probably rather hostile to it. It is true that Jewish family life seems to have been above the average of purity and stability in the early Roman empire, and it is probably a fair guess that the standard of morality was higher in devout Jewish circles, especially in Palestine, than in other communities of the day. But with this there went—this, at least, is the impression gained from the New Testament as well as from such Jewish evidence as is available—a certain repressiveness and prudishness which, upholding high moral standards, did not allow women much freedom, nor men much companionship with women outside matrimony.[10] The impression one gains is that early Christianity gained its high standard of sexual morality at the price of a measure of repressiveness and sometimes at the price of an almost scornful attitude to 'the weaker sex'. One cannot help thinking of the Pauline regulations in I Cor. 11.5 ff. and 14.33[b] ff.—the former passage carefully regulating the decorum of women when they pray in the assembly by prescribing some sort of headdress, the latter apparently prohibiting their uttering themselves at all (notoriously an apparent contradiction). One thinks, too, of the even more absolute prohibition, along the same lines, in the Pastoral Epistles, I Tim. 2.11 f.,

A woman must be a learner, listening quietly and with due submission. I do not permit a woman to be a teacher, nor must woman domineer over man; she should be quiet.

One thinks of the very strong subordination-doctrine (the prelude to the passage just cited) in I Cor. 11.3,

But I wish you to understand that, while every man has Christ for his Head, woman's head is man, as Christ's Head is God.

And one thinks of Tit. 2.4 f.,

. . . school the younger women to be loving wives and mothers, temperate, chaste, and kind, busy at home, respecting the authority of their own husbands.

And, even more significant perhaps, is the strong aversion evinced by Paul in I Cor. 7 from the married estate. It has been brilliantly argued by H. Chadwick[11] that Paul is here exercising very skilful

[10] If this is offensive to Judaism, my main point, at any rate, lies within the Christian traditions themselves.
[11] 'All things to all men', *NTS*, 1.4, May 1955, 261 ff.

tactics against a group of extreme ascetics, with whom he is not himself in sympathy, by making the maximum concessions to their point of view only in order to restrain their zeal by refusing to accept their ultimate principles. But it is difficult, I think, not to feel that Paul is himself genuinely out of sympathy with the married estate. And even the more liberal and genial passage in I Peter 3.7 does not go very far towards a positive estimate of womankind.

Not that one can deny that a new concern for women and a new tenderness towards them marks these very passages. It is precisely in I Cor. 7 and 11 that Paul makes his famous statements about the mutual interdependence of man and woman:

The wife cannot claim her body as her own; it is her husband's. Equally, the husband cannot claim his body as his own; it is his wife's. (I Cor. 7.4).

And yet, in Christ's fellowship woman is as essential to man as man to woman. (I Cor. 11.11).

And one cannot but trace such insights to the influence of the Lord himself. But all this does not add up to the impression of an environment in which one can conceive of the Gospel portrait of Jesus being created. On the contrary, the Gospel portrait of Jesus would seem to have fairly forced its way through an atmosphere still to that extent alien to it and still scarcely comprehending. Jesus, who was not afraid of earning the reputation of being a gluttonous man and a wine-bibber, a friend of tax-collectors and sinners, emerges in the Gospel traditions as one who risked obloquy also for consorting with disreputable women; and the extraordinary thing is that writers who must themselves have hated and feared the very risks they are describing and who were themselves not wholly free from a repressive attitude, yet, despite themselves, succeed in presenting a strangely convincing picture of Jesus—a young, unmarried man—allowing himself to be fondled and kissed by such women, without either embarrassment or acquiescence in their morals. The simplicity and sure-footedness of the delineation are amazing. Jesus simply accepts these women as persons: compassionately and with complete purity and simplicity he accepts their affection while moving them to repentance. Thus he establishes at once God's judgment on their standards of life and his mercy towards them. All the quite varied traditions in all four Gospels tell the same story, whether it is the story of the Samaritan woman at the well in John 4, or the delicately drawn scene in the (perhaps Lucan) *pericope adulterae* now in John 8, or the Synoptic anecdotes in Luke 7.36 ff., Mark 14.3 ff., and the parallels in Matthew and John.

Jesus and Israel

There is another feature of the ministry of Jesus, to which Dr G. B. Caird[12] has recently called attention as one which asserts itself despite a demonstrable lack of concern for it in the Evangelists themselves. This is his message to Israel. Dr Caird, arguing that the Evangelists have well preserved much tradition concerning Jesus which they were not themselves particularly interested in or concerned with, concentrates, in particular, on his attitude towards his own nation. Many scholars—especially, in recent times, J. Jeremias[13]—have already written about Jesus' temporary concentration on Israel, and his hopes of a wider mission thereafter. Dr Caird's special contribution is the recognition that Jesus, in his preaching, presented his own ministry as a national crisis—as God's challenge to Israel to fulfil its destiny of being God's dedicated servant. The alternative was disaster for Israel—political disaster. Yet, if Israel as a whole does not respond, God's purpose will not be ultimately frustrated, because there is an already assured nucleus of true Israel, namely, the Twelve and, perhaps, other close associates who had responded. It is only when Israel is its true self, responding to God and fulfilling its destiny, that the Gentiles also will come in. Thus, Jesus proclaimed a 'spiritual' message with a political relevance, a nationalist message with a universal consequence. In his Pelican Commentary on St Luke,[14] Dr Caird writes in the same vein:

The missionaries [that is, the Seventy, sent out by Jesus according to Luke 10.1] are bidden to fulfil their task with the utmost haste; they are to carry not even the simplest impedimenta, to avoid the time-consuming futilities of oriental wayside etiquette, to waste no time on

---

[12] *Jesus and the Jewish Nation*, the Ethel M. Wood Lecture for 1965, University of London, Athlone Press, 1966.
[13] *Jesus' Promise to the Nations*, ET, SBT 24, 1958, of *Jesu Verheissung für die Völker*, 1956.
[14] *St Luke*, 1963, 142 f.

the heedless, and to leave behind them any scruples they may have about the ritual cleanness of food, which would certainly hamper their effective progress. Their mission is an urgent one because they are harvesters: Israel is ripe for the sickle and must be gathered into the garner of the kingdom while the brief season lasts. . . .

The judgment of Jesus is pronounced against whole towns and cities, which implies that he is now looking for a corporate rather than an individual response to the gospel message. He has come to recall Israel to her true vocation as the holy people of God, and the cities of Israel must choose between his way of humble, self-denying service and the other way of defiant and contemptuous nationalism. Again and again in the succeeding chapters we shall find Jesus warning Israel that to reject him is to choose disaster on that day—the day when God's transcendent judgment takes historical form and is worked out by human agents of destruction.

It is this, Dr Caird thinks, that explains many otherwise unexplained aspects of the Gospel tradition, including the acceptance by Jesus of the Baptist's rite of Baptism, the urgency of the mission of the disciples in Luke 9.1 ff. and 10.1 ff. and the fact that the post-resurrection Church had to learn the idea of universalism by experience.

If Dr Caird is right, here is another example of this phenomenon of a tradition forcing its way through a generation which had itself forgotten its relevance and perspective.

Amen

Another straw in the wind which seems to be blowing in the same direction is, again, a Semitic word embedded in the Greek of the New Testament, namely *amen*. It is a remarkable fact that the traditions of the words of Jesus in the Gospels represent him as using this Semitic asseveration at the beginning of a clause: 'Amen, I say to you . . .' or (as St John's Gospel has it) the double form, 'Amen, amen, I say to you . . .'. It is frequently observed that, whereas it is easy to find in Jewish literature examples of 'Amen' at the end of a clause, or simply as a response to something uttered by another, there is no known non-Christian example of its use as a particle for opening a statement. The evidence is in Strack-Billerbeck's *Kommentar*, I (1922), 243 f., and *Jewish Encyclopaedia*, I, *s.v.* 'Amen', adduced by D. Daube in *The New Testament and Rabbinic Judaism.*[15] In this study, Daube

---

[15] *The New Testament and Rabbinic Judaism* (Jordan Lectures, 1952), published 1956, 388.

offers ingenious speculations to the effect that it may, nevertheless, have been a genuinely non-dominical usage but have been
later submerged or rejected; but there seems to be no direct
evidence for this. And, what is more, the strange usage of *amen* as
an opening particle is not perpetuated even in the Christian usage
of the rest of the New Testament. So far as the evidence goes, then,
it looks like a usage unique to Jesus himself. And it does not seem
to me to be straining the evidence when two such different scholars
as E. Käsemann and G. E. Ladd both fasten on it as one of the
indications of Jesus' extraordinary sense of personal authority.
'. . . what is certain', writes Käsemann in his famous paper on
'The Problem of the Historical Jesus',[16] 'is that he regarded
himself as being inspired. This we can gather above all from the
remarkable use of the word "Amen" at the beginning of important logia, which has been so faithfully preserved by the
Evangelists. . . .' 'Jesus' use of the word to introduce a statement',
writes Ladd,[17] 'is without parallel in rabbinic usage. Jesus used
the expression as the equivalent of an oath, paralleling the Old
Testament expression, "As I live, saith the Lord". Jesus' usage
is without analogy because in his person and words the Kingdom
of God manifested its presence and authority. H. Schlier is right[18]:
this one little word contains *in nuce* the whole of Christology.'

There are clauses in the Apocalypse beginning with 'Amen'
(7.12; 19.4; 22.20), but these all turn out to be liturgical responses.
They do not introduce a statement, as in the dominical sayings.
And the use of the responsive 'Amen', 'through Jesus Christ', in
II Cor. 1.20, already alluded to, only confirms that Christians,
knowing of Jesus' exceptional usage, refrained from it themselves,
and preferred to adhere to the ordinary Jewish *amen*, adding,
however, 'through Jesus Christ'.

The Twelve

Thus, a phrase of Jesus'—preserved, as it would seem, despite,
rather than because of, later Christian usage—adds its witness to
the sense, already conveyed by the Gospel narrative, of a breath-

[16] First given at the reunion of Marburg old students on 20 October 1953.
First published in *ZTK*, 51, 1954, 125 ff. ET in *Essays on New Testament Themes*
(ET, SBT 41, 1964, of *Exegetische Versuche und Besinnungen*, I, 1960), 15 ff.
(see 41 f.).

[17] *Jesus and the Kingdom*, New York, 1964, London, 1966, 163.

[18] *TDNT*, i, 338.

taking assumption of authority by Jesus. Of this quiet but decisive assumption of authority, one signal example must now be mentioned, if only because it seems, somehow, often to escape notice: Jesus chose the Twelve. Why twelve? If we are right[19] in accepting a corporate, collective interpretation of the Son of Man, there seems to be a sense in which Jesus identified his closest circle of friends with himself in his vocation and mission. It might not, therefore, have been altogether surprising if he had chosen not twelve but eleven associates, so as to make up, with himself, the symbolical true Israel.[20] But he chose twelve. Can this mean anything else than that he saw himself as standing over this band of associates, as himself above and outside the true Israel, even when he identified his own mission with the mission of Israel? Is Jesus tacitly assuming towards the nucleus of the reformed and re-created Israel the position of God himself *vis-à-vis* his People? If this is so, an implicit Christology of great height has come through from the traditions, in a shape which is the more striking when some Christians were speaking of Christ as the Head of a Body which was his People. If anything, the Gospel hint indicates an even 'higher' Christology than this, but one, at the same time, which was wholly implicit, not explicit at all. It will not do, I think, to argue that Jesus chose twelve besides himself merely because he knew that he would soon be removed by death. Had he no inkling of the impending removal of others, too, by death—let alone the loss of Judas?

Elijah

There is another phenomenon rather similar to this, to which I want now to draw attention. It may be suitably introduced by an observation by a distinguished contemporary German scholar who has already been quoted. E. Käsemann[21] is greatly impressed by the humility with which Jesus sets the Baptist alongside of himself in the famous saying in Matt. 11.12 f.:

Ever since the coming of John the Baptist the Kingdom of Heaven has been subjected to violence and violent men are seizing it. For all the

[19] See above, pp. 34 ff.

[20] On numbers in the Qumran sect, see B. Reicke in *The Scrolls and the New Testament*, ed. K. Stendahl, 1958, 151; and E. F. Sutcliffe, 'The First Fifteen Members of the Qumran Community: a Note on 1QS 8.1 ff.', *JSS*, 4, 1959, 134 ff.

[21] See *Essays on New Testament Themes*, 43.

prophets and the Law foretold things to come until John appeared, and John is the destined Elijah, if you will but accept it.

Käsemann comments:

The situation in this epoch is that the kingdom of God has already dawned, but is still being obstructed. The Baptist has introduced it, and thus ushered in the turning-point of the aeons. Yet even he still stands in the shadow of him who now speaks and utters his 'until today'. Who but Jesus himself can look back in this way over the completed Old Testament epoch of salvation, not degrading the Baptist to the position of a mere forerunner as the whole Christian community and the whole New Testament were to do, but drawing him to his side and—an enormity to later Christian ears—presenting him as the initiator of the new aeon?

But Käsemann continues as follows:

But who then is this, who thus does justice to the Baptist and yet claims for himself a mission higher than that entrusted to John? Evidently, he who brings with his Gospel the kingdom itself; a kingdom which can yet be obstructed and snatched away, for the very reason that it appears in the defenceless form of the Gospel.

Now, the phenomenon I have in mind is comparable. It is the identification of John the Baptist with Elijah. The standard remark among New Testament scholars is that here the Synoptists represent a different tradition from that of John. In the Synoptists, we are told, John is identified with Elijah, whereas the Fourth Gospel, in straight contradiction, represents John the Baptist as expressly rejecting the identification: ' "Are you Elijah?" "No", he replied' (John 1.21). But this is a misleading presentation of the facts, which are more subtle. We have to ask *by whom* the identification is made, and *by whom* refused. The Synoptists represent *Jesus* as identifying, or comparing, the Baptist with Elijah, while John represents the *Baptist* as rejecting the identification when it is offered him by his interviewers. Now these two, so far from being incompatible, are psychologically complementary. The Baptist humbly rejects the exalted title, but Jesus, on the contrary, bestows it on him. Why should not the two both be correct? It is true that, if so, the Synoptic tradition is, for some reason, silent about John's repudiation of the title; but it may well be the Fourth Evangelist's anxiety to stress that the Baptist's rôle is essentially only that of witness and nothing more that has led to the presentation by him of this one half of a tradition only.

After all, selection is often at work on the traditions; and I see no reason to reject a tradition merely because it appears in only one stream, provided it is not intrinsically improbable or contradicted by the other.

But we can go further. If the Baptist really did reject the Elijah claim, it means that he was refusing to accept a rôle equivalent to messiahship. Elijah was an eschatological figure, equivalent to the Messiah. It must be remembered that, in Malachi 4.5 (Hebrew 3.23), Elijah precedes, not the Messiah but the Day of the LORD. Elijah is not the Messiah's forerunner, but the Messiah's equivalent: he ushers in the Day of the LORD.[22]

Why, then, did Jesus, on the contrary, insist that the title of Elijah did belong to the Baptist? Did it mean that Jesus, so far from himself claiming messiahship, bestowed this status on the Baptist? Perhaps the answer to that is 'Yes' and 'No' simultaneously. Jesus, I believe, did not (as is sometimes said) actually repudiate the title 'Christ' for himself, though he appears not to have sought or claimed it until the triumphal entry and the trial. The triumphal entry and the trial do, I believe, represent affirmations of the messianic title, but then, at the same time, they represent a spiritualizing of it. It is no nationalist rebel kingship but a great affirmation of the spiritual Lordship of God over Israel, and an attack, not on the Romans, but on religious abuses at the heart of Israel's sanctuary.

And insofar as Jesus did accept messiahship he not only 'spiritualized' it in this sense, but exalted it in a transcendental sense. The use of Ps. 110 in Mark 12.36 (which, despite opinion to the contrary, I see no reason to regard as impossible on the lips of Jesus himself) indicates the exaltation of the status: if Christ, yet also more than Christ—David's Lord.

Thus, it is arguable that Jesus conceived of John as Elijah (which places John on the level of the Messiah as ordinarily conceived), but saw his own function as equivalent not to the Messiah as ordinarily conceived but to more than the Messiah—indeed (and this is my main point), to that which Elijah (or the Messiah) heralds. Elijah heralds the Day of the LORD. If Jesus' herald, John the Baptist, is Elijah, then the coming of Jesus himself is

---

[22] This point has often been observed before. See e.g., J. A. T. Robinson, 'Elijah, John and Jesus: an Essay in Detection', *NTS*, 4.4, July 1958, 263 ff. Reprinted in *Twelve New Testament Studies*, SBT, 34, 1962, 28 ff.

tantamount to the coming of the Day of the LORD. Is, then, the rejection of the Elijah-title by John a modest refusal to accept messianic status—and also, perhaps, a refusal fully to recognize the status of his successor; and the bestowal of the Elijah-title on him by Jesus a tremendous, though concealed, acknowledgment of the divine, crisis-bringing character of his own ministry? And, if so, has this startling piece of 'high' Christology come through the traditions unostentatiously, almost unnoticed, asserting itself in the narrative before ever its significance was brought out into the open? I would not, myself, like to assert that this is the true account of the reason for the phenomenon. But the phenomenon is there, and deserves pondering.

Baptism

There is one further example of continuity-phenomena, which may be displayed before conclusions are drawn. I refer to the interpretation of baptism in the New Testament. The New Testament interpretation of baptism is striking, to say the least. Probably there is no commoner or more widespread phenomenon in the religions of the world than the ritual use of water. It would be difficult to find any religion in which it does not play some part. And nothing is more obviously symbolized by the ritual use of water than cleansing. Lustration almost universally symbolizes purification. How remarkable it is, then, to find that in the New Testament, although purification is indeed associated with baptism, an equally, if not more, prominent meaning attaching to it is *divestiture* of all that is evil, even to the length of self-surrender in death—death and burial with Christ, and resurrection with him into the power of life! The Qumran sect—which presents a picture of religious practice in a community close, in time and place, to the origins of Christianity—evidently used water-rites extensively (though, in meaning, they were ritual rather than moral[23]), and also (like Ezekiel at an earlier period) applied the idea of cleansing with water, as a metaphor, to the drastic purgation which the Spirit of God was expected to bring about in the future:

Then God in his truth will make manifest all the deeds of man and will purify for himself some from mankind, destroying all spirit of perversity, removing all blemishes of his flesh and purifying him with

[23] See M. Black, *The Scrolls and Christian Origins*, 1961, 98.

a spirit of holiness from all deeds of evil. He will sprinkle upon him a spirit of truth like waters of purification. . . . [24]

In the same way, John the Baptist seems to have associated his baptism with the most drastic purgation and repentance: he used water with a view to repentance, and associated it with the greater purgation which was to be brought by his successor—'He will baptize you with the Holy Spirit and with fire' (Luke 3.16). But even here, there is no real parallel to the Christian associations. If we wish to see the matter in perspective, we may first collect the New Testament references to baptism as purification, and then note how far the New Testament goes beyond this idea. Excluding the Gospels, to which we shall turn in a moment, here are the purificatory passages:

Acts 22.16 (Ananias to Paul):
Be baptized at once, with invocation of his name, and wash away your sins.

I Cor. 6.11: . . . You have been through the purifying waters.

Eph. 5.25 f.: Christ . . . loved the church . . . cleansing it by water and word.

Titus 3.5: . . . he saved us through the water of rebirth . . .

Heb. 10.22: . . . our guilty hearts sprinkled clean, our bodies washed with pure water.

I Peter 3.21: Baptism is not the washing away of bodily pollution . . . (implying that it *is*, in some other sense washing).

II Peter 1.9: he has forgotten how he was cleansed from his former sins (probably a reference to baptism).

But, over and above this, there are references associating baptism with death and divestiture:

Rom. 6.3 f.: Have you forgotten that when we were baptized into union with Christ Jesus we were baptized into his death? By baptism we were buried with him, and lay dead, in order that, as Christ was raised from the dead in the splendour of the Father, so also we might set our feet upon the new path of life. . . .

Col. 2.11 f: In him also you were circumcised, not in a physical sense, but by being divested of the lower nature; this is Christ's way of circumcision. For in baptism you were buried with him, in baptism also you were raised to life with him through your faith in the active power of God who raised him from the dead.

[24] 1QS 4.20 f., in A. R. C. Leaney, *The Rule of Qumran and its Meaning*, 154.

In I Peter 3.21 the water itself is indeed prominent, but its meaning—significantly—is not washing but *drowning*:

This water [i.e. Noah's flood] prefigured the water of baptism through which you are now brought to safety . . . [that is, as Noah's flood drowned the evil world leaving only the faithful, so baptism kills and drowns, in each individual, all that is evil in him].

Now, whence, we are bound to ask, did this extraordinarily powerful and drastic conception of baptism arise? Look in the Gospels, and you find the accounts of how Jesus himself submitted to baptism at the hands of John. What is their most distinctive feature? It is that the baptism of Jesus is closely associated with a divinely conveyed vocation of obedience. It is with the baptism that the Gospels associate a unique dedication of Jesus as Son of God; and with this, in turn, goes the story of the temptation, which hinges on the unqualified, unreserved obedience of perfect sonship over against its Satanic parody of self-concern. And, in its turn, this filial obedience is brought to its climax and fulfilment in the death of Jesus. More than this, death is metaphorically spoken of, in two sayings of Jesus, as baptism:

Mark 10.38: . . .Can you drink the cup that I drink, or be baptized with the baptism I am baptized with?

Luke 12.50: I have a baptism to undergo, and how hampered I am until the ordeal is over!

If, then, we are asking, How did Paul and others come to associate baptism not merely with purification, but, more drastically, with death? the answer is ready to hand. There are, of course, the mystery religions, so beloved of those who try to derive Paulinism from paganism. But there is nothing in the mystery religions and the cult of the dying and reviving Nature-gods (even if it were plausible to suppose that Paul was in close enough touch with these to draw upon them) which is anything like as close to the Pauline doctrine of baptism as Jesus himself is. Already, the baptism of Jesus himself was bound up with his utterly obedient death, which led through to the resurrection with power. Death, burial, resurrection, and the powerful release of the Spirit of God—this striking sequence is in Jesus, before it is in Paul. And if baptism is, in one of its aspects, the relating of an individual adherent to the community of Christ, it is intelligible that it must be a relating of him to that whole cycle of events which, in Christ, had led through to life and power—a cycle in which the total surrender of death was central.

So decisive is the relation to Christ that it has been plausibly argued that the formula baptism 'into Christ' or 'into the name of Christ' is a new, Christian construction. If so, as has already been suggested in an earlier chapter,[25] the unique formula, baptism 'into Moses', in I Cor. 10.2, is not to be taken to indicate that, after all, 'into Christ' means no more than 'as a disciple of Jesus' (as one might call the Israelites disciples of Moses). Rather, it is to be explained as a rare construction derived, by analogy, from the Christian experience rather than *vice versa*. This is the view put forward by Dr C. K. Barrett,[26] and it seems to me, on the whole, more plausible than Dr G. R. Beasley-Murray's attempt[27] to level down the 'into Christ' formula so as to mean no more than what the Mosaic formula by itself might be assumed to mean.

Here, then, is one further illustration of the way in which, at every turn, Christian devotion and Christian faith in the risen and exalted Lord are bedded deep in historical traditions. The 'event' seems always to be basic.

If we look back over the phenomena displayed in this chapter, they will be seen to be broadly of two types. First, there is Luke's careful distinction between the scene of the Gospel and the scene of the Acts. He portrays the contemporaries of Jesus as not using the explicit titles of reverence and adoration for Jesus which he does represent the early Church using. In other words, Luke's treatment of his story—without our begging any questions about its reliability or authenticity—exhibits an awareness of a difference in the attitude of observers towards Jesus as between these two periods; and this gives the lie to the notion that the Church's estimate of Jesus is something which Christians unconsciously adopted in the course of time, and then simply assumed as having obtained from the beginning. Instead, it must either be that Luke has cunningly devised a theory of a 'concealed' Lord who was destined to be revealed later (which, as I have argued, is an improbable theory); or else, some event

[25] See pp. 38 f. above.
[26] *From First Adam to Last*, 1962, 49 f.
[27] *Baptism in the New Testament*, 1962, 128 f.

really did occur after the death of Christ which precipitated the change in recognition.

But, secondly, we have witnessed the reverse phenomenon. Aspects of Jesus' attitude and ministry have survived in the traditions, despite the fact that the early Christians do not seem to have paid particular attention to them or recognized their Christological significance. These bear witness in a subtle and paradoxical way to the identity of the Jesus of the ministry with the Lord who was worshipped, and to the tenacity and continuity of the traditions about him.

V

CONCLUSIONS

I HAVE displayed select phenomena from the New Testament. I have chosen them, not on the basis of orthodox source-criticism, which treats certain sources (Q and Mark) as superior to others; nor on the basis of so-called 'form-criticism', which adopts certain procedures to reconstruct the earliest form of a tradition. I have chosen them, rather, as phenomena which simply call out for some explanation; and I have asked, What do they mean? And I have made no secret of the sort of answer which seems to me to be the only adequate sort. Their meaning— to take them in the order in which they have been displayed— might be summed up as follows. First, whoever tries to account for the beginnings of Christianity by some purely historical, non-transcendental event, runs up against the difficulty that there seems to be no such event of sufficient magnitude or of a kind such as to fulfil the need. It is like the gentleman living in that two-dimensional country, Flatland, for whom the passing of a sphere through his country would be an event causing two-dimensional phenomena so disturbing that his orthodox, two-dimensional language would prove inadequate, and the need to grope after a new understanding in terms of an added dimension would become urgent, even if he had nothing but the language of symbol and myth with which to do the groping.[1]

Secondly, whoever tries to interpret Jesus as only an individual of past history, instead of as a somehow inclusive being, is confronted by phenomena of language and experience whose origin then defies explanation.

Thirdly (grouping the remaining phenomena under a single heading), whoever deems that the conception of Jesus as standing in a unique relation to God is a figment of pious imagination,

[1] See *Flatland: a Romance of Many Dimensions*, by A. Square (Edwin A. Abbott), 3rd revised ed., 1926.

must explain how it came to be constructed, with almost inconceivable and apparently unpremeditated ingenuity, so as to be to such a degree coherent and subtly consistent with itself. Or, again, to account for the portrait of Jesus in the Gospels by postulating that the Evangelists disregarded history and simply constructed a figure out of their current experience and imagination, is to ignore the very remarkable relation between the Jesus of the earliest traditions and the Jesus of the Church's faith—a relation exhibiting both continuity and difference.

But supposing all these points are conceded to the maximum: what then? Is this at all a substantial contribution to Christian apologetic? Even if it is not naïvely credulous (as some of my own colleagues in New Testament research will hold), has it got us anywhere? Supposing that not merely these, but many more points could be firmly established, is this going to make the slightest difference to Christian faith? Is not faith faith? Can faith stand or fall with the establishment of historical events or of a hiatus which seems to postulate a trans-historical event? What, anyway, are events, and what is history—let alone the 'trans-historical'?

I am bound to say that here I gratefully take my stand with Professor Cullmann, over against the Bultmann school, in his insistence on the inseparability of event from decision. These two are not always thus held together. Some scholars who welcome the kind of factual emphasis I have been making tend, in their Christology, to be much closer than I am to the old Liberal Protestants; and, conversely, some whose Christology I would endorse tend to be much less concerned with what I would call history. But I find myself driven to have it both ways, and, if I interpret him correctly, I can appeal to Dr Cullmann's authority for support in this. Not that we deny the distinctiveness of faith. Decision there must be if there is to be Christian faith. Faith is faith, and no amount of photography or tape-recording of events could compel it. To see is not necessarily to believe. But, on the other hand, neither is *blind* faith real faith. For belief it is necessary to see—at least something. The decision to accept Jesus as Lord cannot be made without historical evidence—yes, historical— about Jesus.[2] If it were a decision without any historical evidence

---

[2] Cf. N. A. Dahl in *Kerygma and History*, ed. Braaten and Harrisville, 161: 'The fact that Jesus can be made an object of historico-scientific research is given with the incarnation and cannot be denied by faith, if the latter is to remain true to itself.'

it would not be about Jesus (a historical person) but only about an ideology or an ideal. Even 'bare kerygma' is not basis enough for a Christian decision, if that kerygma includes no more history than the death of Jesus of Nazareth. To be sufficient it must include more. We need to know what manner of man Jesus was. We need to know how he fitted into the religious history of Israel. Some character sketch and some tradition of his sayings and his judgments and his values and some estimate of his relation to the past is integral to the proclamation that evokes decision. That is why the Gospels and the Old Testament scriptures are needed to give content to the bare proclamation. We may decide to embrace a proposition, such as that God is one; or an ideal, such as that all men should be brothers. But before we can decide for Jesus we need to know what manner of man he was, how he was related to his antecedents, why he died, and what (so far as it can be indicated) lies behind the conviction that he is alive. To take all this unexamined is not Christian decision at all, even if it may be a moral or a religious decision.

And therefore, the alternatives are not either mere history coupled with a rationalistic estimate of Jesus as a very good man (an estimate such as could be made by an atheist), or commitment to a preached but unauthenticated Lord. Christian commitment is a commitment of faith and worship indeed, and it is commitment to a transcendental Jesus who is Lord and God; but it is all this in the light of evidence about the character of this Jesus and about his credentials as Lord and God, and about the genesis of the Christian conviction. The creed is not a series of assertions made in a vacuum, but a summary of value-judgments reached on the basis of eye-witness testimony to an event. For the event to which that testimony is borne refuses to be fitted into either the purely rational and particular or the purely abstract and general. It is particular, yet transcendental. To cut out the event is, therefore, either to turn gnostic or else to turn rationalistic; for the event, if my display of phenomena is an honest one, refuses to be reduced to the wholly rational; and yet, the transcendental value-judgments mean nothing that is distinctively Christian if they do not attach to the event.

If, then, the event is basic, that is why we can never dispense with critical examination of the evidence and constant re-assessment of its value. Something in history lies at the heart of faith. But faith it is—because the more we prove and test, the more this thing in history refuses to be bound down to a merely rationalistic interpretation. It is the careful illustration of this that is the strength of that small book, *The Riddle of the New Testament* (originally published in 1931), by the late Sir Edwyn Hoskyns and Mr Noel Davey. Its arguments need, to my mind— I hope it is not impertinent for me to say so—a good deal of revision and qualification and restatement. Its conclusions, as far as I can see, do not invariably follow from its data. But it was one of the very few works of British biblical scholarship at the time which succeeded in making any impression on Continental theologians, however justly critical they were.[3] And I believe the reason is, as I have said, that its thesis was this substantially sound and immensely important one: the nearer you push the inquiry back to the original Jesus, the more you find that you cannot have him without a transcendental element. What you find is not a rationally intelligible person of past history, but a figure who, although a figure of actual history—datable, placeable—emerges as the fulfilment and crown of a long process of divine education of Israel, and as the one who precipitates decision and brings the Kingship of God to bear on all his circumstances. Here is history which only coheres and makes sense when it is interpreted as 'Salvation-history'.

And it seems to me that we stand today once more at the parting of the ways. Recent theological writing has tended to dismiss the importance of history in favour of the transcendental call to decision; or, alternatively, to dismiss the transcendent in favour of such history as can be confined within the categories of purely human comprehension. But I cannot see how a serious student of Christian origins can concur with either. It seems to me to be at once the most striking and the most disquieting character of the Gospels that they steadily refuse to be settled in either direction. On the one hand, the old Liberal Protestant way of stripping off the transcendental and rendering the Gospels rationalistically intelligible is widely agreed to have proved to be a *cul de sac*; and its repetition by those who try to present Christian doctrine without transcendence has no advantage over it, as far as I can see, except a more modern sound. On the other hand, a Gospel which cares only for the apostolic proclamation and denies that it either

[3] See W. G. Kümmel, *Das Neue Testament*, 1958, 519.

can or should be tested for its historical antecedents, is really only a thinly veiled gnosticism or docetism and, however much it may continue to move by a borrowed momentum, will prove ultimately to be no Gospel.

And that is why, as it seems to me, Christian historical apologetic, for all its outmodedness, really needs no apology. It is to one corner of that sort of apologetic that these sketches purport to be a contribution; for they attempt simply to display a selection of the phenomena which need to be reckoned with, and to ask, What do you make of these? Can you make sense of them as history without importing precisely the value-judgments to which the original Christians were led? Conversely, can you account for the value-judgment without the historical basis?

Appendix I

FROM DEFENDANT TO JUDGE—AND DE-LIVERER: AN INQUIRY INTO THE USE AND LIMITATIONS OF THE THEME OF VINDICATION IN THE NEW TESTAMENT*

THE intention of this paper is to establish that the figure of the one who is rejected but is ultimately vindicated is even more widely used in the biblical presentation of the Gospel than is sometimes recognized; while, at the same time, that figure is not as adequate as is sometimes suggested for representing the essential ministry of Christ. In particular, the inquiry will involve a reconsideration of certain aspects of the much-debated figure of the Son of Man, and an attempt to indicate its limitations in this very respect, that this vindication-theme attaches to it more readily than any distinctively redemptive associations. In making this latter point I wish without further delay to acknowledge that I shall only be reiterating what has been already said by others— for instance, recently by Professor T. W. Manson.[1] But my further challenge to the frequently made assumption that the figure of the Suffering Servant of Isa. 53 is fused with that of the Son of Man *in the traditions of the sayings of Jesus* and in the thought of the primitive Church generally has not (I think) been heard so often in recent years.

I omit many examples of the vindication theme which might be cited. But two judgment-scenes in the Old Testament of a more extended nature call for particular notice: one—from early post-exilic times—is the trial-scene in Zech. 3 where Joshua the High Priest is vindicated against an opponent (*hassaṭan*, ὁ διάβολος),

* Reprinted, by kind permission of the Syndics of the Cambridge University Press, from *Bulletin of the Studiorum Novi Testamenti Societas*, No. III, 40–53 (first published, 1952, reprinted by Cambridge University Press, 1963).

[1] 'The Son of Man in Daniel, Enoch, and the Gospels', *Bulletin of the John Rylands Library*, 32, No. 2, March 1950.

who is rebuked. The other is the famous law-court scene of Dan. 7, where the faithful Jews, persecuted under Antiochus Epiphanes, are vindicated before God. To both of these we shall have to return later.

But now observe that a vindication-scene, comparable both to the Zechariah 3 and the Daniel 7 ones, appears to underlie Ps. 110 (and cf. Ps. 2), where God vindicates some lordly figure against his enemies and (mark the parallel to Zechariah) designates him High Priest, confirming it with an oath; while the end of the Psalm magnifies this individual's vindication up to a national scale and speaks of some decisive victory in battle. In the course of the Psalm, the vindication is spoken of in terms of the subjection of enemies beneath the feet of the triumphant one: and this, in its turn, is reminiscent of Ps. 8, with its exclamation of wonder at the fact that God has subjected creation beneath the feet of feeble man—the son of man.

We have now moved from the vindication of a defendant in a lawsuit to that of a warrior on the battle-field, or of one part of God's creation over the rest—evidence of the way in which different themes and a variety of different metaphors cross and overlap and interlace; and it would be ridiculous to suggest that, in such a welter of ideas, there is any coherent *literary* connexion between the various *documents*. All I wish to stress is that there is a common fund of thoughts behind them, and a chain of linked ideas, which runs: obscurity, humiliation, oppression—vindication by God—triumph over subjected foes; and that themes appearing in more than one of these otherwise disconnected passages include those of High Priesthood (or Priesthood), the Law Courts, and humankind—the son of man or one resembling a son of man. Incidentally, it is important for the study of the use of the Old Testament by the New Testament writers to observe how the oracles going now under the name of Zechariah (however diverse in date or origin) include the themes of the vindicated defendant, the priesthood, the shepherd, the martyr, and the king. No wonder the early Church often resorted to those few chapters!

I here omit much evidence which might be adduced for the procedure and the apparatus of law-courts in biblical times. But one element—that of written evidence—is particularly interesting in relation to our main theme. Regrettably, Job 31.35 is dreadfully corrupt; but the last clause may, perhaps, allow a glimpse of an allusion to written evidence in a metaphorical passage (which, precisely because it is metaphorical, must be presumed to confine itself to well-known and recognized procedure when analogy is the aim): thus, *wᵉ sēpher kāthab îš rîbî* seems to mean 'and the scroll which my accuser has written' (so the International Critical Commentary takes it), LXX συγγραφὴν δὲ ἦν εἶχον κατά τινος. The phrase *hen-tawwi*, earlier in the same verse, may refer to 'making one's mark', in a legal deposition. If only we had it all, it might prove to throw considerable light on bonds, and other written evidence, in those days. At any rate, we have Daniel 7.10, which is particularly interesting as an instance of written records in a judgment scene; and with this allusion we may suitably pass over to the working out of the theme of vindication in the New Testament, for the βίβλοι of the apocalyptic scene in Dan. 7.10 take us straight to the New Testament Apocalypse.

Dr Otto Roller, the author of what must surely be the fullest, most ponderous, and most magnificently documented work[2] ever produced on the formulae of ancient letter-writers and their significance for the study of the New Testament Epistles (whatever scholars have thought about his conclusions—and Professor E. Percy has recently pronounced severely against him)[3] was also the writer, shortly before his death, of an article about the roll (βιβλίον), sealed with seven seals, in Rev. 5.[4] He argued that this sealed document could not have been a book (containing the story of the future, or whatever else commentators may have put into it), since no book would be both written on the *verso* (as the βιβλίον of Rev. 5 is explicitly said to have been) and also sealed. On the contrary, he maintained, this sealed 'opisthograph' was clearly a legal document of a type well-attested, though for a limited period, being the equivalent in (I suppose) papyrus or even vellum of the well-known double clay tablet, comprising a legal document securely sealed against falsification, with a duplicate copy outside for easy reference. But if a legal document, it cannot be a will (a proposal made by Zahn, which Schrenk in *TWNT* still seems prepared to entertain), for a will was always a single document, not an opistho-

[2] *Das Formular der paulinischen Briefe*: Beiträge zur Wissenschaft vom alten und neuen Testament, ed. A. Alt, R. Kittel, 5. Folge, Heft 6, Stuttgart, 1933.
[3] *Die Probleme der Kolosser- und Epheserbriefe*, Lund, 1946, 10 ff.
[4] 'Das Buch mit sieben Siegeln' *ZNW*, 36, 1937, 98–113.

graph. This seven-sealed opisthograph can be, argued Roller, nothing else than an indictment, a legal deposition; and the breaking of the seals and the reading of the authentic inner copy is the authoritative act of Christ who is the Judge. The breaking of the seals is the initiation of the process which in fact occupies the rest of the Apocalypse—the judgment and condemnation of the sinful world; and it is as a preliminary to this great judgment that the redeemed People of God are rescued and vindicated against their Accuser, the κατήγωρ (12.10, 12). If this immensely ingenious interpretation breaks down, I suspect it is because apocalyptic is characterized not by logical consistency but by multiple symbolism. It may be perfectly true that in real life a roll which was not only inscribed on its outside as well as inside but also sealed, would be instantly recognized as nothing else than evidence for an indictment; but it is also true that to seal a roll is an attested phrase, especially in apocalyptic, for concealing or temporarily reserving a prophecy (Isa. 8.16; Dan. 8.26; 12.4, 9; and cf. Rev. 22.10), and that a roll written on both sides is a symbol of a full book (Ezek. 2.10); and it is in the manner of Hebrew imagery to put two such symbols together without questioning their mutual compatibility on the literal level. But I confess that I am reluctant all the same to abandon Dr Roller's very clever notion out of hand: if he were to prove right, what an arresting detail might be added to our collection of law-court imagery in the presentation of the Gospel! However, disregarding this particular point, the Apocalypse is, of course, full in any case of the vindication theme; and it is in keeping with this that Christ appears, at the beginning of the book, as the Danielic Figure who is to come with the clouds to be vindicated in the eyes of all (1.7, cf. 14.14)—the rôle, it may be noted, in which he also appears in the Gospels at the trial before the Sanhedrin. In Rev. 20.11 ff. there is a particularly impressive trial-scene, with the Judge (God himself, apparently) on the Great White Throne, and the books (as in Dan. 7). This time the books are certainly not legal documents: the first mentioned are the records of men's deeds, and that other book, mentioned afterwards, is the book of life in which are enrolled the names of loyal citizens. To both these types of record, commentators are able to adduce plenty of parallel references: for the βιβλία containing a record of men's deeds, Dan. 7.10; Isa. 65.6; Jer. 22.30; Mal. 3.16; Esth. 6.1; ? Jer. 17.1; and add (*si vera l.*), Pss. 40.7 (of destiny?),

56.8; for the Book of Life, Rev. 3.5; 13.8; 17.8; 21.27; Phil. 4.3; Luke 10.20; Heb. 12.23; Pss. 69.28; 139.16 (yet hardly 'of life'); 87.6; Ex. 32.32; Isa. 4.3; Ezek. 13.9; Dan. 12.1; Enoch 47.3; Jubilees 39.6; 19.9; 30.20.[5]

There is no need, then, to labour the elaborately juridical tone of the Apocalypse. But before leaving Dr Roller, this may be a suitable place to note an interesting suggestion thrown out by him in the same article. He brings the χειρόγραφον of Col. 2.14 into the same context of ideas as the seven-sealed roll—namely the ideas of indictment and obligation. The sealed document gains its authority from the properly accredited witness of the inner writing secured against tampering. The force of the *cheirograph* is that it is an autograph written by the accused himself—an 'I.O.U.' which proves him a debtor.[6] There is an actual instance of such a *cheirograph* embedded in Philemon, where Paul writes: 'I Paul write it with mine own hand, I will repay it'. Thus, the *cheirograph* of Col. is an autograph 'I.O.U.', acknowledging that we are under an obligation—that we have undertaken—to keep God's moral law. This it is which proves us guilty (for we have all broken God's law), and which can only be cancelled at the cross by the divine acceptance of the debt (cf. the significant 'to fulfil all righteousness', in Matt. 3.15). How to construe the dative τοῖς δόγμασιν, which follows the word χειρόγραφον, is a notorious problem which need not delay us here, though I gratefully acknowledge the new light thrown on it by Dr J. A. T. Robinson[7] when he suggests that the dative is governed by the idea of subscription to an obligation implied in χειρόγραφον. But before we leave Col., it is possibly worthy of note that the metaphor of *divesting* (for so I take it, although I know there are other possibilities), the stripping off of clothing, occurs (2.15) in this same context. Is it conceivable that the pictorial background is, once more, the passage in Zech. 3, with the High Priest accused in filthy clothing, but vindicated, stripped of his disgrace, and reclothed?[8] It is, perhaps, worth observing that the clothing

---

[5] See Schrenk, 'βίβλος, βιβλίον', *TWNT*, i, 613 ff.; J. A. Montgomery, *Daniel*, International Critical Commentary, 1927; W. Fairweather, 'The Development of Doctrine', Hastings' Dictionary of the Bible; A. Bentzen, *Daniel*, Handbuch zum Alten Testament, 19, 1937, *in loc.*

[6] For parallels to the idea of an accusing document, see E. Stauffer, *New Testament Theology*, 1955, n. 463.

[7] 'The Body', SBT 5, 1952, 43 n. 1.   [8] Cf. J. B. Lightfoot, *in loc.*

and crowning (or 'mitring') metaphors of the Zech. 3 scene come to the surface elsewhere also: see Ps. 109.19; and in Ps. 132.16, 18ᵃ one finds this metaphor both *in bonam* and *in malam partem*; and then follows the 'mitring', v. 18ᵇ. Regarding this latter, it has even been suggested that, on such an occasion, for instance, as the establishing of the covenant between Jehovah, king, and people at the coronation of Jehoash, a copy of the agreement was actually bound round the King's head like a turban (see II Kings 11.12). If so, possibly the very obscure Job 31.36 may indeed be (as the International Critical Commentary had long ago suggested) a reference to a similar habit of binding an agreement upon the head. Job 31.35 has already been adduced, in connexion with written evidence; and the whole passage, vv. 35-37, might be found relevant to the procedure in the case of trial for insolvency, were it not that the text is bankrupt! At any rate, the main point is that divesting of shameful garb, reinvesting splendidly, and sometimes also crowning or mitring (mitring even with a symbolic document), were evidently ideas associated with the vindication of God's cause—sometimes in the person of a Priest-King (with Rev. 1.13 cf. Zech. 3.4).

Returning now to the New Testament and to the main theme, we have to consider the place of the figure of the unexpectedly vindicated one, and, in particular, of the Son of Man as a symbol for this idea. One thing may be said at once—that the association, both of the Human Figure of Dan. 7 and of the Son of Man in the Gospels, with *clouds* is itself intended to mean exaltation, triumph, vindication, and, indeed, to represent the dramatic reversal of rôles from defendant to judge. One used to be told that in Dan. 7 the *coming with clouds* meant not *descent* but, if vertical movement at all, rather *ascent*: that it, in fact, was a pictorial allusion to a triumphal *exaltation* of the oppressed people. Bentzen (*Daniel*, p. 30) and others now deny this: it is, after all, the descent from heaven of a pre-existent Figure (or—with T. W. Manson, *op. cit.*—of a pre-existent Idea or Ideal). Certainly in the Apocalypse (1.7) where the coming with clouds is combined with the martyr-vision from Zech. 12 (a combination also illustrated by Matt. 24.30), it is clearly a *descent*—the second coming, in fact. But I am inclined, myself, to think that when the New Testament writers alluded to the Danielic clouds, they were in any case more interested in the exaltation, the glorification, of the Son of Man than in his ascending or descending as such: I mean, that one may say that broadly ἀνάστασις, ἀναβαίνειν, ὑψωθῆναι, δοξασθῆναι, and μετὰ τῶν νεφελῶν all shared, as their primary association, the idea *vindication*, whether or not there was a secondary eschatological reference. *Ascension* is a comparatively rare theme in the New Testament (nowhere, for instance, is it to be found in the assuredly Pauline writings, as C. L. Mitton[9] reminds us); but the *resurrection* itself is equally clear evidence of vindication; and so is δόξα. So that whether Christ is *glorified* in the transfiguration or demonstrated to have *risen*, or spoken of as *ascended*—it is all one in regard to his credentials as the vindicated one (cf. I Tim. 3.16, though I do not think that *the Spirit* is there instrumental in vindicating, as is argued for other passages below). And it is, accordingly, a daring paradox of *realized* eschatology when it is asserted that the Son of Man hath authority to forgive sins (judicial authority) *upon earth—before* his vindication; and an even more daring piece of spiritual evaluation to see the Son of Man's true ὕψωσις in the exaltation on the cross. And I suggest that when Jesus is represented as saying before the Sanhedrin that he is the Christ (or at least not denying it—even if Matthew's 'Thou hast said' and Luke's refusal to reply are regarded as non-committal), the meaning of the additional words (in all three versions and variant forms) is that it is as the exalted, vindicated, kingly *Christ* that the oppressed *Son of Man* will directly be seen (Matt. 26.64, Mark 14.62, Luke 22.69). It is, in fact, another way of equating the Son of Man (*when vindicated*) with God's Chosen One. Exactly in the same vein is John 8.28: 'When you have (by condemning him) "exalted" (on the cross) the Son of Man, then you will find out that I am (the Vindicated Messiah).' In different terms, the same *process* is reflected in Rom. 8.30: 'whom he called' = the elect; and these are *vindicated* and *glorified*. So too Acts 17.31, where 'God will judge the world in righteousness by *the man* (= the Son of Man) whom he hath ordained (= the elect); whereof he hath given assurance unto all men, in that he hath raised him from the dead (= glorified and so vindicated)'. So, too, Rom. 1.3, 4; and cf. Luke 18.7, 8 (the vindication of the elect).

This compels me to allude back, once more, to the Old Testament; for it is of some moment in this connexion whether the

9 *The Epistle to the Ephesians: its authorship, origin and purpose*, 1951, 204.

suffering and eclipse of the Human Figure is or is not an important factor in the scene of Dan. 7. There is no need to discuss here the degree to which that chapter is composite (Bentzen, p. 33, etc.). All that matters for the present purpose is the text as used and read in the time of Christ; and I confess I find it difficult to ignore or discount (with some commentators) the clear allusions to eclipse and defeat followed by vindication and kingly status, in vv. 21, 22. As the chapter stands now (whatever the stages of its composition) *the saints are symbolized by the Human One*—not identified with, but represented by him: and if the saints are partially and temporarily eclipsed, only to be subsequently glorified, then exactly the same may be presumed to be appropriately predicated of the Human Figure. *If so, then 'the Son of Man' already means 'the representative of God's chosen people, destined through suffering to be exalted'*; and I would question whether it is not a little misleading to read[10] in Vincent Taylor '. . . although a time of conflict is described in Dan. 7.21, 25, it is from Isa. 53 that the darker colours in the portraiture are derived'; and (still more sweepingly): 'It is not, of course, written anywhere that the Son of Man should suffer. The question [i.e. Mark 9.12[b]] . . . implies the identification in the mind of Jesus of the Son of Man and the Suffering Servant of Isa. 53.'[11] In his recent commentary, Dr V. Taylor[12] writes (on Mark 14.21): 'There is no Old Testament passage (except Dan. 7.21) in which the suffering destiny of the Son of Man is affirmed. Only, therefore, in the mind of one who has identified the Son of Man with the Suffering Servant is the saying intelligible. . . .' But does not 'as it is written of him' make the case for a reference to Dan. 7.21 the stronger? Note also that W. D. Davies[13] accepts Dan. 7 as indicating a *suffering* Son of Man. It is true that the Fourth Evangelist evidently takes a different view of current expectation, when he makes the people say 'We have heard out of the law that the Christ abideth for ever [cf. Dan. 2.44 and 7.14]: and how sayest thou, The Son of man must be lifted up? who is this Son of man?' (12.34); but he also, in the same sentence, represents them as using ὑψωθῆναι in a *sinister* sense, which seems so unlikely to have been what they

---

[10] *Jesus and His Sacrifice: a study of the passion-sayings in the Gospels*, 1937, 90.
[11] *Op. cit.*, 94.
[12] *The Gospel according to St Mark*, 1952.
[13] *Paul and Rabbinic Judaism*, 1948, 280.

actually did that the whole saying becomes obscure and difficult to use as evidence—except in one respect, that it apparently assumes the identification of the Son of Man with the Christ.

Be that as it may, the application of 'the Son of Man' to Jesus seems to mean that it at least represents his expectation of victory through suffering, vindication after defeat. But it means more than being vindicated: it means vindicating; for on any showing the term is to this extent a collective one that the person of Jesus is representative, inclusive, incorporative; and therefore if his cause is vindicated, then with it he becomes the *Vindex* of the body of people whom he represents and sums up. When Daniel's Human Figure comes with the clouds to the divine presence, that means (says the interpretation in the same chapter) that the people of the saints of the Most High are given judgment. The defendant, vindicated at his trial, is discovered to be the judge; and Matt. 25 can quite naturally speak of the Son of Man coming to hold a great assize upon the nations. As Jesus is ἀρχηγός, πρόδρομος—the forerunner and pioneer for his people—so also he is their Vindicator, in the sense that in him is already realized the ultimate vindication of his Body the Church. This is illustrated (with an interesting limitation) in Luke 18.1-18 (the parable of ἐκδίκησις), where it seems that the elect who are to be vindicated when the Son of Man comes are those who have faith. Cf. 21.28, though note that in v. 36 even the elect are under judgment also.

It is in connexion with this function of Vindicator that I want to put forward two suggestions—one small and trivial, the other possibly of rather more importance. The first is this. In the account of the death of Stephen, the martyr sees the Son of Man standing at the right hand of God. Quite apart from the very striking fact that this and the Apocalypse references are the only occurrences of the Son of Man theme outside the Gospels, it has often been remarked that the *standing* posture is significant; but in what sense? In the sense (so it is said) that Christ is seen in the act of rising to his feet to welcome his witness Stephen.[14] What I suggest is rather that the standing posture is itself (as has already been illustrated from the Old Testament) that of a witness (add *Ascens.*

[14] Dr E. Stauffer has pointed out to me, however, that the 'welcoming' interpretation at least has support from a coin of the Ascension of Constantine with the hand of God stretched to welcome him; so in the Dura Europos pictures of the crossing of the Red Sea, God's hands are visible.

Isa. 9.35, 36, though here 'on the left'); and the Son of Man is here portrayed giving decisive evidence in vindication of his oppressed disciple—even the position at the right hand of God may (accordingly) be juridical no less than princely.[15] In short, this is a double trial scene, exactly as is the scene in which Jesus witnessed a good confession before Pontius Pilate (I Tim. 6.13) or before the Sanhedrin. Just as there Christ is condemned by the human court but declares that the Son of Man will thenceforth be exalted with the clouds and vindicated, so here Stephen is condemned and put to death, but in the heavenly court, where the books have been opened, this member of the Son of Man community is already being vindicated by the head of that community —*the* Son of Man *par excellence*; and as Stephen's witness confessed Christ before men, so Christ is standing to confess him before the angels of God. It is the more significant, if so, that the martyr with his dying words begs the heavenly court for mercy towards those against whom he is vindicated.

The other suggestion is (as I say) of rather more importance. It is that 'paraclete' in the Fourth Gospel is best interpreted if we take its primary connotation to be uniformly that of *Advocate*. This is not only a literal rendering (*advocatus*), avoiding the linguistic violence done to the form of the word by other proposed equivalents, but makes, I believe, the *best* sense of the notoriously difficult passage 16.8–11, makes at least *good* sense of 15.26, 27, and does not conflict with the other passages (N.B.—ὀρφανοί, 14.18, are precisely the class for whom a *goel* was proverbially needed); is in exact keeping with the use of the word in I John 2.1 (where incidentally the paradox of the law-courts is recalled by the phrase 'Jesus Christ the righteous', and further coupled with the striking term ἱλασμός); and is illustrable (as Bengel remarked) from the story of the Acts. I am not, of course, suggesting that the Fourth Evangelist is likely to have intended the word in only one sense: if there is any one obvious characteristic of his manner, it is that he uses a word suggestively, as a poet may, with any number of associational overtones,[16] and I am not forgetting that Luther and the Authorized Version ('Tröster' and 'Comforter') are very deeply rooted in our affections. Nor am I ignorant of a most able

[15] See E. Stauffer, *New Testament Theology*, n. 446. [Add, now, p. 60 above.]
[16] See O. Cullmann, 'Der johanneische Gebrauch doppeldeutiger Ausdrücke,' etc., *Theologische Zeitschrift*, 1948, 360 ff,

presentation before this Society only three years ago of the case for a decidedly different interpretation.[17] All I wish to submit is that to treat *Vindex*, *Advocatus* as the dominant note of this word makes very good sense and harmonizes the thought with a great deal else in the Bible. The exaltation of the Son of Man declared in the trial scene of the Synoptic Gospels is, on that showing, closely to be related to the era of the Paraclete—that is, the period when the early Christian community was vindicated against its opponents and detractors (as is described in the Acts) by the signal witness of the Holy Spirit within it. It is when Jesus is *glorified* (as the Fourth Gospel itself says) that the era of the Spirit begins; it is when exalted to the right hand of God that he pours forth 'this which ye do see and hear'. The heavenly intercession of the exalted Christ (in Heb. and Rom. 8) is much the same theme, although in Heb. the ἐμφανισθῆναι before the divine Presence (9.24) is *priestly* rather than *juridical* (unlike the perhaps technical φανερωθῆναι—appear in court—of II Cor. 5.10). The Priest is himself also *Vindex* of his people (cf. the 'High-Priestly' prayer).

Thus it is that, according to Acts 17, Jesus has been appointed judge of the world, with the resurrection as his credentials; and by derivation, the Christian Church can also be spoken of as destined to be Judge (Matt. 19.28; Luke 22.30; I Cor. 6.3). Thus, the people of the saints of the Most High turn out to be both vindicated and also, thereby, able to pronounce judgment; and this Danielic thought is picked up in Rev. 20.4 and applied explicitly to Christian martyrs.

It is sometimes said that the Fourth Gospel is, in its use of 'the Son of Man', at least on the way to that later sense of the term in which it means humanity rather than supernatural majesty. But I doubt if the famous saying about all judgment being committed unto Jesus because he is the Son of Man (5.27) will bear this sense. Is it not more probably an allusion to the Danielic Son of Man whose destiny is to rise from defendant to judge (cf. I Enoch 69.27)? Cf. John 12.31–33 (already adduced above), where judgment and exaltation come together.

But of course *ultimately* the two conceptions do coincide; for the exalted Son of Man *is* humanity as humanity is meant by God to be (Ps. 8, Heb. 2); and humanity, finally brought to maturity in the redeemed Christian Church, will exercise the judgment

[17] See C. K. Barrett, *JTS*, n.s. 1, 1950, 1 ff.

alluded to in I Cor. 6. This reminds us that, whatever may be the reason for the term 'the Son of Man' dropping virtually out of currency after Christ's use of it, St Paul makes use, instead, of the terms ἄνθρωπος and *Adam*. I confess that I find it difficult to follow Dr W. Manson when he takes 'the Son of Man' to have been a term of the universalist world-mission represented by Stephen as against the Judaizers.[18] If he is right, it seems to me more difficult than ever to account for the way in which the term recedes out of sight in the Paulines. Recede it does, whatever the reason. Is it, possibly, because there were better words than 'Son of Man', when once the Son of Man had been glorified—'Christ', 'Lord', 'Son of God'; and a less ambiguous term for his common share in humanity—ἄνθρωπος or *Adam*? That is, the Son of Man, *on earth*, is predominantly thought of as *to be vindicated in the future*; and when once he is actually *with the clouds* then a more exalted title is suitable; cf. Wisd. 2.18, suggesting that a real 'Son of *God*' is regarded as essentially a vindicated and triumphant figure. At any rate the vindication theme remains: the new humanity, the saints, the sons of God—whatever terms St Paul uses to describe those who are in Christ—have been vindicated by the death and resurrection of the one who was seen in human form (σχήματι εὑρεθεὶς ὡς ἄνθρωπος) and has been very highly exalted. Indeed, when one comes to think of it, the very terms of Phil. 2 are themselves not far from Danielic: ἐν ὁμοιώματι ἀνθρώπων and σχήματι εὑρεθεὶς ὡς ἄνθρωπος—what are these phrases if not equivalent to 'like unto a son of man'? (So Stauffer[19] speaks of the Apostles as explaining the Son of Man sayings by new figures.) And what is the exaltation at the end of that passage but a variant of the coming with the clouds? Vindication after eclipse is here, exactly as in Dan. 7; and in the vindicated one the people of God are also vindicated, as is stated in so many words in the great trial-scene in Rom. 8. We have to remember that the Eighth Psalm is never far from the mind when a New Testament writer is thinking about Christ in his representative capacity as the true humanity, the new Adam; and just as Heb. 2 specifically applies Ps. 8 to the ideal, victorious, vindicated humanity of Christ, so Rom. 8 has, as part of its background, the yearning frustration of all creation because of the failure of humanity to reach God's

---

[18] *The Epistle to the Hebrews: an historical and theological reconsideration*, 1953, 31 etc.   [19] *New Testament Theology*, 26 f.

glorious purpose for it—the purpose summed up in the one word δόξα; and it dwells also on the corresponding hope that that purpose, having actually been achieved in Christ, will ultimately be achieved in man; and so to the stately, rhetorical passage, vv. 29-34. There you have, once more, the familiar law-court terms: Christ, humiliated only to be exalted; at the right hand of God, pleading in the heavenly court for those who are his people on earth. It is Isa. 50.8, 9 transposed into a Christian key.

By this I do not wish to imply that St Paul's use of δικαιοῦν and the related words is primarily concerned with vindication. I believe that in some passages these terms have moved so far from a verdict of acquittal or even a triumphant vindication of the oppressed as to be interpretable rather in terms of putting right a spoilt relationship—in short, that δικαιοῦν is often nearer to καταλλάσσειν than anything else; and that this use of δικαιοῦν to denote a personal relationship restored is probably the most characteristic one in the Paulines. But, if so, it remains true that here and there, at the very least, the original vindication theme protrudes, and here, in Rom. 8, is one example. Another is possibly in Rom. 4.25, where the much disputed phrase *might* I think, mean that Christ was raised from death because of *our* vindication—because a verdict of 'not guilty' was ours before the heavenly court, as soon as Christ, our representative, had suffered under the adverse sentence. At any rate—to turn to secondarily Pauline writings—in II Tim. 4.7, 8 we find a games metaphor apparently fused with a law-court one, when reference is made to the Assize Day, the Just Judge, and the vindicating verdict, which is also the wreath awarded to the *victor ludorum*.

But indeed the illustration of this theme is not really a matter of drawing out a quotation here and a verse there: for it is of the very texture of the New Testament. Instead of wearying you, therefore, with a long list of references, let me simply remind you that *miracles* are widely regarded by the New Testament writers as *vindications* of the power and presence of God, just as the supreme miracle, the resurrection, is treated as the supreme credentials of Christ's status. βεβαιοῦν is, as Deissmann and Preisigke have shown,[20] a juridical word; and if God is said to establish his

[20] A. Deissmann, *Bible Studies*, ET 1901, 104 ff. (see Arndt and Gingrich, *A Greek-English Lexicon of the NT*, 1957); F. Preisigke, *Fachwörter des öffentlichen Verwaltungsdienstes Ägyptens in den griechischen Papyrusurkunden der ptolemäisch-römischen Zeit*, 1915, *s.v.*

message by the signs which attended it ([Mark] 16.20), that is precisely how miracles are regarded throughout the New Testament. Thus it is that the rejected stone is vindicated, the sacrificed lamb becomes the lion of Judah, the advocate Spirit vindicates the oppressed and suffering people of God, the one on trial turns out to be the Judge: an immense variety of expressions all converging on the same theme—vindication.

Instead of elaborating this theme further, it is time to turn to one which, by contrast, is conspicuous for its astonishing rarity in the Bible, namely, that of the rescue, by the vindicated one, of his own opponents. The dramatic reversal of the rôles by which the condemned becomes the condemner—the prisoner in the dock turns out to be, after all, the judge upon the *bema*—this is common enough; but the third step, from judge to Saviour, is very rarely found in the form 'Saviour *of his enemies*'. That the vindicated one achieves, in his own vindication, the vindication or rescue also of the oppressed people whom he represents is a commonplace (as we have seen) of biblical thought. But where are the people who condemn the innocent spoken of as saved by the innocent one when he is vindicated over them? Answer—nowhere in the Old Testament, unless it be in Isa. 53. Everybody knows how desperately obscure that celebrated oracle is, and the more intimate one is with the text, the less (I expect) one feels prepared to dogmatize. But this much does appear to be tolerably clear— that the Hebrew text describes the utmost surprise on the part of onlookers, on discovering that someone whom they had assumed to be suffering under the displeasure of God had in fact been the innocent sufferer under a chastisement which actually belonged by right to them; so that whereas they had at least 'consented unto his death', if not actively joined in his condemnation, they now discovered that it was by that very death that they—who themselves deserved it—had been rescued and reprieved. This is astonishing. The righteous sufferer is a familiar figure; so is the righteous sufferer vindicated; but the unrighteous oppressor rescued from his evil ways through that vindication—was anything so illogical ever heard of or hinted at before? So far as one can see, the answer is no, nor yet after—unless it be in that moving passage in the Pentateuch where it is implied that Moses' self-surrender might somehow help to restore the guilty people (Ex. 32.32).

But this idea is not only rare in the Old Testament. In the New Testament too, how strikingly seldom it comes to full expression! Anybody who reads the New Testament at all knows, of course, that the principle is stated in so many words in Romans (especially chapter 5) and in other parts of the Paulines and in I Peter and the Johannine writings: we have already noted in I John 2.1, 2 the coupling together of δίκαιος (the vindicated one) and παράκλετος (the vindicator) with ἱλασμός (the expiation); but in the Synoptic Gospels, although we can see, in retrospect, how the whole life of Jesus is directed to this end, it is very rarely enunciated; and even in the traditions of the sayings of Jesus himself it is exceedingly rare. It is a commonplace of the interpretation of the Gospels to say that the Messianic idea was drastically modified by Jesus by the use of the title 'the Son of Man'; and that 'the Son of Man' is, in its turn, subtly fused, in the mind of Jesus, with the figure of the Suffering Servant. (Dr M. Black reminds me of the possibility that Dan. 12.3 at least had already been influenced by Isa. 53.) But how little *direct* evidence there is for this last step, and how smaller still is the specifically *redemptive* application of this concept! It is a well-known fact that, apart from the possible allusion to Isa. 53 in the famous ransom saying (and even this is not clear), and perhaps the Words of Institution (and observe that even these, unless one is convinced that the simple reference to sacrifice 'for the sake of *many*' must be an allusion to the words of Isa. 53, are far from *verbally* close, however close they are in *theme* to that chapter), there is no allusion in the recorded sayings of Jesus to the redemptive work of the Servant. If I am right in holding that 'the Son of Man' meant primarily the persecuted but ultimately to be vindicated one, then it is a curious thing, in itself, that Jesus adopted for himself a title with such severe limitations— a title which required such a violent wrenching in the direction of Isa. 53 before it could be really serviceable as a vehicle for his intentions; and still more curious that there are only such slight traces of this necessary wrenching process.

Yet no: that last phenomenon is *not*, after all, so curious, and may, indeed, be the clue to explaining the facts. The reason, I suggest, why explicit references to the redemptive aspect of Isa. 53 are so rare is simply that it was itself so astonishing and difficult that it had not penetrated the early Church's consciousness to any considerable degree. Nothing is clearer than that the kind of

preaching represented by the Acts threw all its stress upon vindication rather than redemption; and if baptism meant being saved,
it was not nearly so clear that it also meant being committed to
saving. We cannot help observing that even the continuous quotation of two verses from Isa. 53 in Acts 8 stops short (perhaps significantly) at the Servant's deprivation of justice; and that not only
in Rev. 1.7 but also in Matt. 24.30, the Dan. 7 passage is conflated
with Zech. 12.10 ff., underlining the martyr's vindication as the
uppermost idea in the interpretation. Similarly in John 8.28 the
nation's exaltation of the Son of Man (on the gibbet) is, ironically,
their vindication of him against themselves. That vindication was
a very difficult idea to dissociate from the Son of Man is made the
more evident when it is recognized that the same continues to be
true of the later vision in II Esdras 13 of the Man from the Sea
(cf. Rev. 1.16; 2.12, 16; 19.15); and that, even in Isa. 53 itself, the
redemptive element is comparatively small as compared with the
'vindicative'. Here I realize that I speak specially subject to
correction, for Dr Stauffer's chapter in *Theologie und Liturgie*[21]
refers to several writers whom I have not been able to consult on
this matter. But before reading it I had written that whatever
evidence may be detected by the brilliant work of Jeremias in
favour of Isa. 53 having been messianically applied before the
time of Christ,[22] and however true it is that Enoch 37–71 shows
signs of Servant and Son of Man having already been fused
together,[23] it remains true also that the *redemptive* motif is lacking:
'it seems clear that the author of the "Parables" [in Enoch]
identified the Servant with the messianic Son of Man. At the
same time it is doubtful whether he fully realized the implications
of the identification, since *there is nowhere any hint* [*in Enoch*] *that
the Son of Man is to suffer*.'[24] Similarly H. W. Robinson reminded
us[25] that Jeremiah, who in many ways was the nearest of all the
prophets to Jesus, was nevertheless terribly vindictive. The
upshot of this seems to me to be that the term Son of Man
was, in itself, as much implicated with kingship, nationalism,

---

[21] *Theologie und Liturgie*, ed. L. Hennig, 1952.
[22] See *Aux sources de la tradition chrétienne: mélanges offerts à Maurice Goguel*,
1950, 114. Also W. Zimmerli and J. Jeremias, 'The Servant of God', SBT
20, revised edition 1965.
[23] See e.g., C. R. North, *The Suffering Servant in Deutero-Isaiah*, 1948, 7, 8.
[24] C. R. North, *loc. cit.*
[25] *Redemption and Revelation in the Actuality of History*, 1942, 271.

vindication, as was the term Messiah, and (as I have already said) I cannot follow Dr W. Manson in seeing its relevance (in itself) to a universalist mission.

We may perhaps have to admit, therefore, that we are not much nearer to understanding why Christ himself seems to have adopted it as his chief title—except that it is at least more germane to suffering than the term Messiah. But we cannot help also recognizing that St Paul and some of the others did grasp the redemptive significance of the death of Christ; and I feel myself driven to the conclusion that it was rather through what Christ *did* than in anything that he *said* that the lesson was learnt—when, indeed, it was learnt. Dr V. Taylor[26] calls the Servant Idea 'this master-key supplied by Jesus himself' and contrasts the very rare use of it made by St Paul; but, as I see it, he is nearer to the truth when (p. 272) he writes: 'There is strong evidence in the Gospels that Isaiah 53 influenced His thought, but it may well be that it was independently of that Scripture that He surpassed the prophet's originality, as perhaps the allusive character of his Old Testament references indicates.' Similarly Jeremias asks[27]: 'But does the originality of Jesus really lie in his having advanced a new messianic theory, as, on this showing, the first to combine Isa. 53 with Dan. 7? Does it not lie rather in his having himself lived out and fulfilled the content of these two scriptures?'

It may be precisely because Jesus left behind him no explicit reinterpretation of the vindicated one in terms of the redeeming one, but relied upon his own life and the power of his Risen Presence in the Holy Spirit rather than on a tradition of teaching, that the early Church, with mighty exceptions like St Paul, often missed the point. To quote Dr V. Taylor once more, he maintains that '. . . the ideas of the King Messiah and the Suffering Servant have been combined. In this combination the thought of primitive Christianity has followed that of Jesus Himself; but with this difference, that whereas Jesus interpreted the Son of Man in terms of the Servant, early Christian thought conceived the Servant in the power and dignity of the Lion of Judah.' It is the latter half of this statement which seems to me manifestly true. Is the first half—about the combination of the Servant and the Messiah in

---

[26] *The Atonement in New Testament Teaching*, 1940, 97.

[27] *Aux sources de la tradition chrétienne: mélanges offerts à Maurice Goguel*, 113 (my own translation).

the thought of Jesus—true only of the *work* of Jesus, or is it true also of his *words*? Can we even be certain that the ransom saying in Mark 10 and the Words of Institution are so much Isaianic as general? Jesus only occasionally *spoke* of his *redemptive* work; when he did, it is questionable whether he drew on the words of Isa. 53. But his work *was* redemptive. It was his work and person rather than his words or his quotations which brought this home.

THE INTENTION OF THE EVANGELISTS*

THE great scholar in whose honour this essay was offered might well have found in it much with which to disagree. But there are at least aspects of it which he would probably have supported; and at any rate nothing can alter the fact—whether or not the essay provides evidence of it—that the writer, in common with all present-day students of the New Testament, owes him an incalculable debt.

The view here presented[1] is that, at the time when the Gospels were being written and first used, the Church was well aware of a distinction between 'the Jesus of history' and 'the Christ of faith', to use the modern clichés; and that, insofar as the Gospels were used in Christian worship at all (and we shall have to ask how far, after all, that was the case), they filled a place broadly comparable to the narrative parts of the Hebrew Scriptures in the Synagogue, as the historical background against which the interpretative writings might be read. The interpretative writings for the Synagogue, one may presume, were, in the main, the Latter Prophets and many of the Writings; for the Christian Church, mostly the apostolic epistles or homilies. The Gospels, it will be here suggested, fall not so much into this latter category as into the former: they were in intention less interpretation, liturgy and

---

* Reprinted, by kind permission of the Manchester University Press, from *New Testament Essays: Studies in Memory of T. W. Manson*, edited by A. J. B. Higgins, 1959, 165-79.

[1] For a most interesting view of the origin of the Gospel tradition—different from that here advanced, but at more than one point relevant to this investigation—see H. Riesenfeld, *The Gospel Tradition and its Beginnings* (an address at 'The Four Gospels' Congress, Oxford, Sept. 1957). See also the communication read by Bishop R. R. Williams at the same Congress in *Studia Evangelica*: papers presented to the International Congress on 'The four Gospels in 1957', ed. Kurt Aland, F. L. Cross, Jean Daniélou, Harald Riesenfeld and W. C. van Unnik (Texte und Untersuchungen zur Geschichte der altchristlichen Literatur, 73, 1959).

theology than narrative statement. It is just possibly this distinction which lies at the back of Ignatius' words (however highly charged they may be with other associations besides) in *Philad.* 5: . . . προσφυγὼν τῷ εὐαγγελίῳ ὡς σαρκὶ Ἰησοῦ καὶ τοῖς ἀποστόλοις ὡς πρεσβυτερίῳ ἐκκλησίας. So, *ibid.* 9, he writes: ἐξαίρετον δέ τι ἔχει τὸ εὐαγγέλιον, τὴν παρουσίαν τοῦ σωτῆρος, Κυρίου ἡμῶν Ἰησοῦ Χριστοῦ, τὸ πάθος αὐτοῦ, τὴν ἀνάστασιν. Lightfoot's very instructive note on the former passage, however, comes down in favour of τὸ εὐαγγέλιον *not* meaning a document, while οἱ ἀπόστολοι means apostolic comment on the events, itself including the Gospels.

Be that as it may, the present trend of thought about the New Testament is, if I interpret it aright, inclined to deny, or at the very least, to overlook, the consciousness of any such distinction in the early Church. We are taught, instead, that even St Mark, let alone the other Gospels, was written 'from faith to faith'[2]: that is, that, so far from being a mere collection of annals, it reflects the religious convictions of the community which was its cradle; that it represents an interpretation of Jesus in terms of Christian conviction; and, in short, belongs rather to liturgy and even to high theology than to history in any of its colder and more annalistic senses. Thus, even one who, like Archbishop Carrington, strenuously denies that the primitive Church had no concern for biography, holds nevertheless that Mark was designed to present Jesus as Son of Man and Son of God and to be read at Christian worship[3]; and here he has a large number of other scholars with him, however little he has carried conviction in the matter of his own 'lectionary' theory of the Gospel.[4]

Now, that the Gospels, or comparable material, had some place in worship who could wish to deny? The analogy with synagogue worship already implies thus much. Indeed, it is virtually demonstrable by the time of Justin, for he speaks (*Apol.* 67) of the reading of the ἀπομνημονεύματα of the apostles at Christian worship, and these 'reminiscences' must have been in some sense evangelic and are indeed actually called Gospels in *Apol.* 66, 3 (though this

---

[2] The phrase is wrenched indeed from its context in Rom. 1.17, and made to mean something quite different. But it is convenient and intelligible in its modern context.

[3] See P. Carrington, *The Primitive Christian Calendar*, 1940, 7, 9 ff.

[4] See the detailed criticism by W. D. Davies in *The Background of the New Testament and its Eschatology*, ed. W. D. Davies and D. Daube, 1956, 124–52.

may be a gloss[5]). Possibly something of the same sort is intended in the command in I Tim. 4.13, πρόσεχε τῇ ἀναγνώσει, though that may well mean the reading of the Old Testament Scriptures. At any rate, nobody could deny the strong probability that from very early times traditions about Jesus were recited or read at Christian worship. We are all familiar with the suggestion that the passion narrative may have been recited at the Eucharist. These Gospel traditions, accordingly, were doubtless framed within the context of Christian faith, so that no Christian writings are mere dispassionate narratives but are documents of faith, springing from such an estimate of the person of Jesus as belongs not to a sceptic but to an already convinced believer.

All this is undeniable, and no one in his senses would attempt to deny it. What may be questioned, however, is any implication of failure, in the primitive Christian community, to realize that there was some distinction in some sense—however impossible it was to draw it in practice—between 'history' and 'interpretation'. Further, it may be suggested that it is a mistake to regard use at worship as the primary function of the Gospels. The Synoptic Gospels, at any rate, are better explained as apologetic material; and even in the context of Christian worship, or of the instruction and edification of Christians, they represent little more than the element of historical foundation—the explanation of 'how it all started'.[6] After all, as to their 'outline' or framework, they are κήρυγμα; and the 'heralding' of the deeds of God in Jesus Christ is, primarily, for the outsider, not for the already convinced Christian: it is evangelistic material; it is propaedeutic; it is that by which a man is first brought within reach of appropriating salvation.

It is only after this, and in the second place, that he is instructed further, and with more particular reference to the Christian *interpretation* of the facts, and is shown how to appropriate what the interpretation implies. Only then is he baptized and brought inside, thus beginning to experience the joint participation in the Holy Spirit. Only then does he find theology real and significant and begin to be nourished by life and worship within the body of Christ. Of course he will go on listening to and reading the nar-

[5] See the late R. G. Heard, in *NTS*, 1.2, Nov. 1954, 122 ff.

[6] It must be freely admitted that Justin, *Apol.* 67, 3, just cited, makes the apostolic reminiscences alternatives to lections not from the Law but from the Prophets.

ratives of how it all began; if he does not constantly return to these foundations, he will never secure the superstructure. But he will not be content with what the Gospels tell him; he will need the sort of theological interpretative matter provided by eucharistic worship and by the writings and sermons of Christian thinkers, in their capacity as prophets and teachers.

Viewed thus, the Gospels (or equivalent material now no longer extant) are first and foremost addressed '*from* faith', indeed, but not '*to* faith' so much as to unbelief. And such St Luke's Gospel, for one, seems explicitly to declare itself. Theophilus has already been instructed; but there is nothing to say that he has yet come inside the Church. The purpose of the Gospel is to possess him of the facts—τὴν ἀσφάλειαν (1.4, cf. τὸ ἀσφαλές, 'the rights of the matter', Acts 22.30; 25.26). Dibelius,[7] while holding that the contents of the Gospel are in a deeper sense εὐαγγέλιον, and were meant also for readers who were already Christians, noted the impartial tone of the exordium; it is as though Luke were announcing a history: Λουκᾶ (Ἀντιοχέως) πράξεις Ἰησοῦ. But if the Gospel is the Acts of Jesus, Dibelius went on to draw a striking contrast between it and the Acts of the Apostles. Holding that the Acts speeches were Luke's own compositions, skilfully designed to point his moral and help to tell his story, he emphasized that in the Gospel, by contrast, Luke contents himself almost entirely with sayings—not speeches—and sayings drawn from the tradition. Thus, a *prima facie* case, at least, can be made for regarding Luke's Gospel as intended primarily to 'tell the story'—and that for the outsider.[8]

The other Gospel which declares its purpose is St John's. It is (20.31) ἵνα πιστεύητε ὅτι Ἰησοῦς ἐστιν ὁ χριστὸς ὁ υἱὸς τοῦ θεοῦ, καὶ ἵνα πιστεύοντες ζωὴν ἔχητε ἐν τῷ ὀνόματι αὐτοῦ. It is, as is well known, possible to interpret this as applying to those who have already come to believe, in the sense that the aim is to deepen or make constant that belief. But perhaps the more natural interpretation (despite the present tense, *si vera lectio*) is that the aim is to evoke belief—to bring outsiders within the fold of the believers. No doubt the other exegesis can be sustained: indeed, the opening

---

[7] *Die Reden der Apostelgeschichte* (*Sitzungsberichte der Heidelberger Akademie*, 1949), ET in *Studies in the Acts of the Apostles*, 1956, 138 ff.

[8] Cf. H. Conzelmann, *The Theology of St Luke*, 1960 (ET of *Die Mitte der Zeit*, 1954), 11 f.

words of I John provide a parallel, and they are clearly addressed to believers. But on the whole, there is a strong case for the view that the Fourth Gospel is more intelligible as a skilful apology to the pagan 'Gnostic' who had heard about Jesus but was misunderstanding him, and perhaps still more to the non-Christian Jew, than as primarily intended for the full believer.[9]

If, then, we may assume for the time being that both Luke and the Fourth Evangelist wrote with more than half an eye on outsiders—or at any rate on those who formed only the fringe of the Church and were not fully inside—what of the other two Evangelists? St Matthew's Gospel never declares its purpose in so many words; but it does not take much reading between the lines to recognize that a large amount of its material would be eminently suitable for pastoral instruction in a Christian community which had come out from Judaism but was still beset by antagonistic Jews at close quarters and therefore required both directly apologetic material and also the narrative of 'how it all began', which is indirectly of great apologetic importance. It looks like ethical and religious instruction designed to equip Christians not only with spiritual help but also with intellectual guidance in facing attack from Jews. All the time it is presenting Christianity as true Judaism in contrast to the spurious Judaism of the anti-Christian Synagogue; and in this regard it is comparable to the Epistle to the Hebrews. It is both conciliatory to the heart of Judaism ('Think not that I came to destroy . . .') and also rigid in its insistence on the *differentia* of Christianity.[10]

Then what of Mark? The most significant fact about it, for the present inquiry, is simply its contents, which are not only within

---

[9] For discussions of this point, see C. H. Dodd, *The Interpretation of the Fourth Gospel*, 1953, 7–9; C. K. Barrett, *The Gospel according to St John*, 1955, *in loc.* and 114 ff.; and, for arguments in favour of a primarily Jewish 'audience', the paper by W. C. van Unnik at 'The Four Gospels' Congress (as in n. 1 above), 382 ff.

[10] I cannot help thinking that this apologetic purpose deserves even more prominence than, e.g., G. D. Kilpatrick's liturgical interpretation suggests (*The Origins of the Gospel according to St Matthew*, 1946). K. Stendahl (*The School of St Matthew*, 1954) agrees that there is material in Matthew, e.g. the 'Church discipline' material, which is not compatible with a purely liturgical use (28). His conclusions (35) might well be extended to make room for the apologetic motive. Incidentally, however, it is perplexing to find, in a Gospel apparently directed to that end, such seeming ignorance of Jewish customs as is implied by Matt. 27.62 ff. (the Jews treat with Gentiles about the guarding of the tomb on the day after *paraskeue*).

the framework of the κήρυγμα[11] but are themselves in the nature of κήρυγμα; and κήρυγμα is primarily the 'propaedeutic' for the outsider. Bishop Rawlinson, in his well-known commentary,[12] described Mark as written 'partly to edify converts, and to satisfy a natural curiosity as to how Christianity began, and partly to supply Christian preachers with materials for missionary preaching, and partly also to furnish a kind of armoury of apologetic arguments for use in controversy with opponents, whether Jewish or heathen'. This seems to be a far more plausible account of it than those which view it first and foremost as liturgically or theologically conditioned. Bishop Rawlinson, it is true, ends the same paragraph by saying that 'the Evangelist's motives were not primarily historical; they were primarily religious'. But 'religious' requires defining; and there are contexts in which religion is best served by the historical. If Professor Cullmann has urged that it is a mistake to postulate two types of Christian worship—a 'synagogue' type and a 'temple' type—at any rate he does allow that it is possible to distinguish a meeting for missionary preaching from a meeting for the edification of the community (despite the fact that an unbeliever may be found wandering into the latter, I Cor. 14.23–25)[13]; and (so, at least, it will be argued directly) it is the *preaching* that is primarily the content of Mark: the κήρυγμα for unbelievers.

Now there were many different types of unbeliever and outsider. Some were Jews, some were devout God-fearers—pagans who had been attracted by the lofty monotheism of the Jews without actually becoming proselytes. Some, if we conjecture aright, were deeply religious inquirers with a background of Hellenistic Saviour cults: not only deeply religious, but capable of understanding such a profoundly spiritual idea as, for instance, the idea of being nourished upon the life of the Saviour and finding life through his death. Others had to be fought with and stood up to: detractors, against whom it was vital that Christians

[11] The sense in which this statement is true may be examined in C. H. Dodd's famous article 'The Framework of the Gospel Narrative', *ExpT*, xliii, June 1932, 396 ff., reprinted in his book *New Testament Studies*, 1953, 1 ff., and D. E. Nineham's criticism of it in *Studies in the Gospels*, Essays in memory of R. H. Lightfoot, 1955, 223 ff. See also my comments on the latter in *JTS*, n.s. 7, 1956, 280 ff.

[12] A. E. J. Rawlinson, *Mark* (Westminster Commentaries), 4th edition, 1936, p. xxii.

[13] *Early Christian Worship*, ET, SBT 10, 1953, 29.

should be armed with polemically effective material. Others again might be described as neutral: they were neither profound, spiritually or mentally, nor yet specially antagonistic: people for whom the first approach to Christianity might be the plain story of what God had achieved in Christ; and if (for the sake of argument) we are classifying the Gospels as though they were addressed, directly or indirectly, to outsiders, it will clearly be this third, 'average' group, for which Mark in particular is the best suited. The cosmopolitan crowds of Rome might well require this type of 'ammunition'.

The words 'directly or indirectly' have been used, since it may now be suggested[14] that Matthew and Mark were both intended chiefly as instruction for *Christians*, though in order to familiarize them with what they needed as equipment for their evangelistic witness to outsiders; while John and Luke were meant as tracts, to be placed directly in the hands of individual readers representing outside inquirers of different types.[15]

But it is time to return to current orthodoxy. Current orthodoxy regarding Mark is, as we know, that it was, in some sense, a composition made up from little narratives and sayings into a structure of great theological significance, for use within the Christian community—perhaps actually at worship; at any rate, largely within the Christian circle, partly for edification, partly to convey theological teaching. After all, the sacraments certainly acted as vehicles of the Christian proclamation: Baptism and the Lord's Supper both represented the shape and sequence of the Gospel; they were epitomes of the Gospel. Why, then, should not the worshipping communities have cast their creed and their theology into the framework of some such narrative as is found in Mark, as well as dramatizing it in the sacraments? That is, *a priori*, plausible enough. Yet, if that was the primary purpose of the Gospels, why did they not include an estimate of the position and status of Christ comparable to that implied by the sacraments and explicitly articulated in the letters of St Paul? Why are they not more credal? And, still more, why is there not some indication as to how Christ might be received and appropriated,

---

[14] Cf. Rawlinson, *ut sup.*

[15] This raises questions, which I am not capable of answering, about the extent to which books or tracts could be produced and multiplied in communities so poor as, for the most part, the Christian communities were.

or, in other words, how incorporation into the Body of Christ took place?[16]

What we have to visualize, it must be remembered, is a community of Christians (say at Rome) who would find it perfectly natural to endorse the little creed at the beginning of Romans (1.3 f.); who would know what was meant by trusting Christ (Rom. 3.22), by having access through Christ to God (Rom. 5.2, 11), by being baptized into his death and fused with him in a death and resurrection like his (Rom. 6.1–11), by being a single body in union with Christ (Rom. 12.5) and by being possessed of and by the Holy Spirit (Rom. 8). Now, if a Gospel like Mark was indeed primarily an expression of the faith of a worshipping community with such an experience and such a creed, and was addressed to its own members, or to those who were in the act of becoming such, how comes it that it exercises such extraordinary —and, on this assumption, misplaced—restraint? It probably (if we accept a well-supported reading in 1.1) twice directly designates Jesus Son of God—1.1, 13.32; otherwise only indirectly— 3.11, 5.7 (demoniacs), 14.61 (the high priest—but perhaps the phrase is only messianic), 15.39 (the centurion), and 1.11, 9.7 (the divine voice at the baptism and the transfiguration). It once (but only by implication) represents him as claiming the title Lord— 12.36; it never calls him Saviour; it only twice alludes to his death as redemptive—10.45, 14.24. It does not get anywhere near suggesting the possibility of disciples becoming more than disciples so as to be living members incorporated in his body.[17] It knows about dying so as to live (8.35), but this is by *following* Christ, that is, by discipleship, rather than by membership, in the post-resurrection manner. Seldom (as is familiar to all students of the Gospels) is there any allusion to the Holy Spirit, and then not in

---

[16] The Fourth Gospel admittedly, though addressed to outsiders (if the suggestion already made be accepted) goes far further to meet this need than the other Gospels. But why should not that be because the outsiders in question were already of a deeply religious cast of mind?

[17] Cf. W. F. Flemington, *The New Testament Doctrine of Baptism*, 1948, 95: 'It was only *after* that Act [the death and resurrection of Jesus] that the rite of Christian baptism could possess its full meaning and potency. Thus we need not feel any surprise that in the Synoptic Gospels there are no passages linking the teaching of Jesus about men as 'sons of God' with baptism. The Synoptic silence about baptism is a measure of the faithfulness with which the records of the ministry and teaching of Jesus have been presented.'

any characteristically Christian sense, but only in ways in which a devout Jew might use it.[18]

It is difficult to understand how such a presentation of Christ could have seemed adequate, if Mark was really intended primarily as a vehicle of praise and meditation for the worshipping Church. Indeed, Mark's εὐαγγέλιον provides a striking contrast to what Professor Einar Molland showed to be the content of εὐαγγέλιον in Paul: '. . . the content of the Gospel is Jesus Christ himself. The heart of the Gospel is the Christological teaching about the pre-existent One who became man to redeem us, and who suffered death on the cross, and who rose again and is at the right hand of God.'[19] In Mark the good news is the good news of the kingdom of God, announced by Jesus; in Paul it is Christ himself offered in the preaching and the worship of the Church. To the same effect are the words of R. Leivestad: 'When we read Mark's story of the passion, we are struck by the remarkable lack of theological interpretation. It is indeed surprising that the Easter tidings could ever be related in this sober, reporting style by members of the Christian Church . . . there is no clear hint at the metaphysical background.'[20]

Why did Mark not go on to portray (as indeed the Fourth Gospel did) the Saviour who gives his life in such a way that we are nourished by it, and whose risen body is that of which we are limbs—the Saviour of Baptism and of the Eucharist? It is not a matter of *disciplina arcani*, for the institution narrative is included. But it is a lack of theology. The Pauline theology which is sometimes claimed for Mark,[21] and which indeed it ought to display

[18] About this Dr E. Schweizer, in *TDNT*, vi, 403, says something very similar to what Mr Flemington, cited in note 17, says about baptism; and see now a short communication on even Luke's restraint regarding 'universalism', read by N. Q. King at 'The Four Gospels' Congress (as in n. 1 above), 199 ff. There are other differences between the Gospel and the Acts which are relevant to our inquiry. [Cf., now, pp. 56 ff above.]

[19] *Das paulinische Evangelion*, 1934, 78 (my own translation).

[20] *Christ the Conqueror*, 1954, 65. I have omitted the following words, as slightly confusing the issue for my present purposes: 'No doubt Mark has written his gospel with the same intention as John, "that you may believe that Jesus is the Christ, the Son of God", but the account of the last hours of Jesus has a strangely sombre and tragic colour. No beams of light from Easter day penetrate the gloom of Good Friday. There is no halo around the cross, no grandeur in the sad countenance of the crucified, and there are no groaning demons.'

[21] Dr Vincent Taylor writes in his commentary: 'Mark's christology is a high christology, as high as any in the New Testament, not excluding that

if it were primarily for the instructed and for use in worship, is uncommonly difficult to demonstrate. The same applies, to take an instance from the other Synoptists, to the Lord's Prayer in Matthew and Luke, containing no word or phrase that is explicitly Christian; and to the Sermon on the Mount, with never a word about the grace of God or about that quality of conduct which is described as ἐν Κυρίῳ. Relevant to this, although in a different context, are Dr Manson's own words[22]: 'It seems a little odd that if the story of Jesus was the creation of the Christian community, no use should have been made of the excellent material offered by one of the most able, active, and influential members of the community.'

Must we not, then, retrace our steps at least part of the way, and examine the ground for a fresh start? Suppose the worshipping communities, as well as 'singing hymns to Christ as God', as well as offering petitions to God in Christ's name, and celebrating sacraments in which they found themselves 'limbs of Christ and linked with one another, also recognized that their faith stood or fell with the sober facts of a story, and that it was vital to maintain the unbroken tradition of those facts? Would they not, from time to time, rehearse the narratives *as such*, first of one incident, then of another, doing their best to keep within the historical limits and not embroider the tale anachronistically, however well they knew its sequel and its inner meaning? Sometimes, obviously, they did embroider and distort, failing to recapture the historical situation. Sometimes, no doubt, they might, in the process, turn aside to underline a hint of something latent in a saying or a deed, which contemporaries had at the time failed to notice, but which subsequent events had exposed and shown to be significant. But sometimes, conversely, may they not have said, 'We would never have dreamed, considering the original facts, that afterwards they would come to be understood so differently'? And in such cases, would they not be all the more careful to keep the story as it was, not spoiling

---

of John' (121); '. . . the ἐκθαμβεῖσθαι καὶ ἀδημονεῖν of 14.33, and the death cry of 15.34, reveal that experience of sinbearing which inalienably belongs to the destiny of the Suffering Son of Man. Ultimately, the Marcan representation belongs to the cycle of ideas which is worked out in the Epistle to the Hebrews, but it has closer affinities with the Pauline doctrine of *In Christo*' (125).

[22] In Davies and Daube (as in n. 4 above), 214 f.

the contrast with what had followed, but rather enhancing it?[23]

It must be reiterated that, of course, this exercise of reminiscent reconstruction (in obedience, perhaps, to a command to remember Jesus) is in no way alien to worship. On the contrary, it corresponds, as has already been observed, to the historical and quasi-historical traditions of the Jews, more particularly to the story of the Exodus which underlay so much of Jewish prophecy, preaching, and worship.[24] But—and this is one of the chief contentions of this essay—it remains in some sense distinguishable from theological deductions, from the preaching of the way of salvation, and from adoration. It is only one ingredient in worship; and its very nature demands that, so far as possible, it be kept in this distinguishable condition and not overlaid by interpretation. And—another point—its purpose accordingly was not only or even chiefly to be used for worship. Still more, it was to equip Christians with a knowledge of their origins, for use in evangelism and apologetic. The real core of worship was the experience of the risen Christ within the Christian Church through participation in the Spirit. But Christians knew well that if they lost sight of the story behind that experience their worship would be like a house built on sand; and that if they preached salvation without the story of how it came they would be powerless as evangelists; and that if they could not explain how they came to stand where they did, they would be failing to give a reason for their hope.

Therefore, they cherished the narrative as something precious. It would be ludicrous to deny that ecclesiastical interests and theological value-judgments ever overlaid the story. It has been as good as demonstrated that they do. But that is not the point. The point is that the Christians knew the difference between the two —between the pre-resurrection situation and the post-resurrection situation—and that their aim was to try to tell faithfully the

---

[23] C. C. McCown, in *The Search for the Real Jesus*, 1940, 305 f., after allowing (what, on my showing, would need to be considerably modified) that the Gospels contain the apostolic faith in an already idealized mystical Christ, goes on to say that they contain 'also a record, meager, but vivid and vital, based upon authentic and largely trustworthy tradition, about a Jesus who actually lived in Palestine nineteen hundred years ago. The Gospels are not merely cult ritual, catechism, and *Kerygma*. They contain all three, but also unimpeachable reminiscence.' I would only question how much 'cult ritual' there is, and whether 'unimpeachable reminiscence' is not itself part of the *Kerygma*.

[24] Cf. Neh. 9, where it is actually woven into a prayer. But see n. 6 above.

story of how the former led to the latter. And in actual fact, they succeeded better than is often allowed.

Two instances may not unprofitably be recalled. First, the saying about fasting in Mark 2.18 ff. and parallels. There can be little doubt that the primitive Church practised fasting: the Acts and the *Didache* are sufficient witness to this. So much so that it has naturally been suggested that the words 'The days will come when the bridegroom is taken away from them, and then they will fast on that day' are an addition by the early Church to justify the difference between their current practice and the non-fasting vindicated by the words of the Lord in the first part of the section. But even if this is granted (and it is not necessarily so), that only underlines the probability of the first part, at any rate, being genuine history. It appears to serve no 'useful' purpose in the primitive Church as a pointer to correct behaviour or procedure; indeed (on the assumption that the second part is an effort to justify current practice), it seems to have been positively embarrassing and perplexing. It is only 'useful' if it is allowed that the Church recognized as 'useful'—indeed, as vital—the reconstruction and preservation of what Jesus said and did in his ministry, *as distinct from* what the Holy Spirit was saying and doing at the time of narration (cf., of course, I Cor. 7.10, 12).[25] Secondly, may one dare to interpret the much-debated saying about parables in Mark 4.10–12 (with or without Dr Manson's Targumic explanation of v. 12)[26] as likewise free from the doctrinaire distortions of the Church? May it not merely mean that nobody can receive the mystery of the kingdom of God without exercising his own responsibility to respond to it? Those who are outside, οἱ ἔξω, are not a fixed, unalterable class: they are merely those who, for lack of response, are at the time remaining 'outside'. In Mark 8.18 the Twelve themselves are in that class. At any time when a man has ears without hearing, he is 'outside'; whenever he listens, responds, and begins to ask for more, he is beginning to be within reach of the mystery. If that is what is meant, it is entirely conceivable within the historical ministry of Jesus. As for the linguistic difficulties in vv. 13–20, there seems to be much truth in the contention that they they are by no means fatal to the substantial

[25] See O. Cullmann, *The Christology of the New Testament*, 1959 (revised ed. 1962), 61 f., and the literature there cited.
[26] *The Teaching of Jesus*, 1935, 177 ff.

genuineness of the section.[27] This is not, of course, to ignore the
ecclesiastical origin of the variants in the Matthean and Lucan
versions: it is only to claim that, in its essence, the saying is not
difficult to fit into a place in the ministry of Jesus.

In all this, nothing is further from the intention of this essay
than to attempt the impossible (and, in any case, undesirable)
feat of drawing an *ultimate* distinction between 'history' and
'interpretation'. Of course it was inevitable—especially for the
profounder and more mystical type of mind—that the two should
be seen as ultimately one: and the Fourth Gospel portrays the
earthly story *sub specie aeternitatis*, perhaps for 'Gnostics' who
would be quick to appreciate certain aspects of such a presentation and who were in sore need of conversion, away from dual-
ism, to certain other aspects less familiar to them. But all the time,
it may still be urged, the Christian communities were vividly
aware of the necessity of trying to avoid romancing, and of not
confusing post-resurrection experiences of incorporation in the
Body of Christ with the pre-resurrection process of discipleship—
of following, learning, imitating.[28] This does not mean for a
moment that they wholly escaped the temptation to heighten the
miraculous and to modify the details.[29] But the amazing thing
is not that they have sometimes modified, but that they have
generally resisted so phenomenally well the temptation to read
back into the narrative the contemporary interpretation of Christ;
and was not this due to a conscious resistance to the non-'historical' in the sense just indicated?

It is sometimes observed that the high, theologically developed

[27] See C. E. B. Cranfield in *SJT*, 4, 1951, 398 ff., 5, 1952, 49 ff. Incidentally,
the confusion between seed and recipients is, if anything, a primitive trait,
which I should be prepared to believe is *reproduced* rather than *introduced* in
Col. 1.6, 10. It may be added that the acceptance of the section Mark 4.10–20
as it stands is made simpler if it is recognized that vv. 10–12 may be treated
as a *generalization*. When Jesus was alone those who took the trouble used
to ask for explanation of the parables. To them he used to say that the mystery
was theirs, while for those who stayed outside everything remained only on
the parabolic level (Jeremias' suggestion that this originally meant simply
enigmatic is not cogent). Then, in vv. 13 ff., follows a *specific* instance of
explanation. This accounts for the sudden change from τὰς παραβολάς
(v. 10) to τὴν παραβολὴν ταύτην (v. 13).

[28] Cf. I John 2.24 ff. ὑμεῖς ὃ ἠκούσατε ἀπ' ἀρχῆς, ἐν ὑμῖν μενέτω, etc.

[29] The Gospels were (in the words of H. E. W. Turner, *Jesus, Master and
Lord*, 1953, 31 f.) 'both books for believers by believers and records of a
factual nature about a historical figure. Here is a tension between the subjective and objective side.'

Christology of the Fourth Gospel represented, in a sense, the earliest impulse of Christian preaching, while the Synoptists represent rather a mature reflectiveness, bringing with it a realization that some historical reconstruction of the antecedents had its place in the preaching of the Gospel, as well as a theological presentation of the meaning and power of the contemporary Christ active spiritually in his Church. To say so is not, of course, to reverse the Gospels chronologically, or to imply that the Fourth Gospel was not the crown of mature reflexion: it is simply to stress that the presentation of the power of the Risen Lord is itself an early and immediate instinct of the Christian Church, whereas the reconstruction of the narrative leading up to it is something more deliberately and more consciously undertaken. In any case, it still remains at least possible that even the Fourth Gospel was not primarily 'worship' but apologetic.[30]

What is here argued for, therefore, is that all four Gospels alike are to be interpreted as more than anything else evangelistic and apologetic in purpose; and that the Synoptic Gospels represent primarily the recognition that a vital element in evangelism is the plain story of what happened in the ministry of Jesus. Thus, all four are to be regarded as having been written primarily with a view to the outsider (*from* faith but *to* unbelief or ignorance), although, as has already been suggested, Luke and John are more likely to have been intended to be *read* by the outsider, whereas Matthew and Mark may well represent instruction for *Christians*, with a view to equipping them in their turn for spoken evangelism. Only secondarily, it is here suggested, would a Gospel have been intended for purposes of Christian worship—and, if for such a purpose, then for its more *instructional* side as distinct from its more directly *devotional* side. I have argued elsewhere,[31] indeed, that a good deal of homiletic matter in the Epistles of the New Testament bears traces of the use of the Gospel narratives as illustrative material. And the Justin passage already alluded to (*Apol.* 67) speaks of the president urging upon his hearers the imitation of the good things which had been read about. But even so, this would not be incompatible with the contention that it is worth while asking whether the primary purpose was not simply

---

[30] To allow this is not necessarily to deny that its thought and words themselves spring from worship—even (as has been suggested by some) from the eucharistic prayer and meditation of the celebrant. [31] *JTS*, n.s. 3, 1952, 75 ff.

the maintenance, for apologetic purposes, of the historical story.

The one point in the Synoptics where all attempt at historical narrative seems to be abandoned is in the reference to the *rending of the veil*. This is surely symbolical *in intention*. Is it not as much as to say, 'Here realized eschatology begins'? But until that point is reached, narrative rather than theology is the intention.[32]

It is a familiar fact that St Mark is the first known book of an absolutely new type. May it not be said that it is the result of a conscious desire to preserve the sporadic traditions of incidents and to set them on permanent record for evangelistic purposes, and that, since the outline of the Good News (which we know as the κήρυγμα) was already necessarily in use in Christian preaching (as it had been from the beginning), it was natural to attach these floating units to this already existing framework? Once this was done, it becomes easier to imagine Matthew as compiled for the same purpose but with much more material and with particular apologetic requirements in view; and Luke–Acts and John as written to be *read* by individuals or groups outside the fully convinced Christian congregation—the earliest known written apologies.

When this has been said, it must still be asked exactly how we envisage the ἀπομνημονεύματα fitting into Christian worship when they were so used: Was the passion narrative read at the Eucharist? Was the baptism story read at baptisms? Were there other occasions in the course of worship when other narratives were read? Can we fit any such reminiscing into the picture of I Cor. 14? Or is it, indeed, significant that it is precisely to such a community that the Apostle addresses remarks which suggest that his friends are forgetting the historical in favour of direct revelation? But for the moment, it need only be reiterated that sooner or later the distinction between narrative and interpretation has to be made both in worship and in evangelism: and we gain nothing by assuming that the early Church was indifferent to the distinction, however true it is that, at a deeper level, the two belong inseparably together and are complementary.

[32] Even after this point, it is incidentally remarkable (as C. H. Dodd has observed in *Studies in the Gospels*, ed. D. E. Nineham, 1955, 25) that the post-resurrection narratives in Matthew, Luke and John do not borrow the 'brilliant light' which might so easily have been imported from the traditions of St Paul's Damascus road vision. In the Gospels this is confined to the transfiguration and (in Matthew) the angel of the resurrection.

ABBREVIATIONS

ET	English translation
ExpT	*Expository Times* (Edinburgh)
JBL	*Journal of Biblical Literature* (Philadelphia)
JSS	*Journal of Semitic Studies* (Manchester)
JTS	*Journal of Theological Studies* (Oxford)
NEB	New English Bible
NovTest	*Novum Testamentum* (Leiden)
NTS	*New Testament Studies* (Cambridge)
S-B	H. L. Strack and P. Billerbeck, *Kommentar zum Neuen Testament aus Talmud und Midrasch* (1922–28)
SBT	Studies in Biblical Theology
SJT	*Scottish Journal of Theology* (Edinburgh)
TDNT	*Theological Dictionary of the New Testament* (trs G. W. Bromiley, Grand Rapids, Michigan 1964–74)
ThLz	*Theologische Literaturzeitung* (Leipzig)
ZNW	*Zeitschrift für die neutestamentliche Wissenschaft* (Berlin)
ZTK	*Zeitschrift für Theologie und Kirche* (Tübingen)

The symbols relating to the Dead Sea Scrolls will be found in the books referred to where quotations are made.

INDEX OF NAMES

INDEX OF REFERENCES

1. OLD TESTAMENT AND JEWISH WRITINGS

2. NEW TESTAMENT

3. OTHER ANCIENT SOURCES